An OPUS book

# LINGUISTIC CRITICISM

OPUS General Editors

Keith Thomas
Alan Ryan
Peter Medawar

OPUS books provide concise, original, and authoritative introductions to a wide range of subjects in the humanities and sciences. They are written by experts for the general reader as well as for students.

# Linguistic Criticism

ROGER FOWLER

Oxford   New York

OXFORD UNIVERSITY PRESS

1986

Oxford University Press, Walton Street, Oxford OX2 6DP
Oxford New York Toronto
Delhi Bombay Calcutta Madras Karachi
Kuala Lumpur Singapore Hong Kong Tokyo
Nairobi Dar es Salaam Cape Town
Melbourne Auckland
and associated companies in
Beirut Berlin Ibadan Nicosia

Oxford is a trade mark of Oxford University Press

British Library Cataloguing in Publication Data
Fowler, Roger
Linguistic criticism.—(OPUS)
1. Criticism   2. Linguistics
I. Title   II. Series
801'.95   PN98.L/
ISBN 0-19-219125-X
ISBN 0-19-289111-1 Pbk

Library of Congress Cataloging-in-Publication Data
Fowler, Roger.
Linguistic criticism.
(An OPUS book)
Bibliography: p.   Includes index.
1. Linguistics.   2. Discourse analysis.   3. Criticism.
I. Title.   II. Series: OPUS.
P123.F65 1986   410   85-15418
ISBN 0-19-219125-X
ISBN 0-19-289111-1 (pbk.)

Set by Colset Private Ltd, Singapore
Printed and bound in Great Britain by
Biddles Ltd, Guildford and King's Lynn

# Preface

*Linguistic Criticism* is an introduction to the critical study of discourse; the chief emphasis is on those works of language hailed as 'literary', but I have tried to make it clear that all texts merit this sort of analysis, and that belief in an exclusive category 'literature' or 'literary language' is liable to prove a hindrance rather than a help. I hope this book will be used as a text in courses whose aim is to enrich the whole of students' experience of language in all its modes.

This book is not intended to be an introduction to linguistics as such; some elementary knowledge of linguistics is presupposed, and Section I of the Further Reading lists a selection of linguistics textbooks which are compatible with this work, or important in themselves, and accessible. Section II recommends some other work in linguistic criticism and 'stylistics'. I have very much assumed that readers will use other texts in the field; in some cases I have tried to facilitate entry into other books by deliberate overlap—for example, I have reanalysed some passages treated in Anne Cluysenaar's *Introduction to Literary Stylistics*, a book which I have found extremely valuable in my own classes. All the books listed in the Further Reading are felt to be complementary, or useful background. More specific supporting reading is mentioned in the notes at the end of each chapter, and not listed in the Further Reading.

*Linguistic Criticism* has been a long time forthcoming, delayed principally by time lost since July 1981 in administrative and political work caused by resources cuts in British universities. I am deeply indebted to my colleagues and students at the University of East Anglia for support given during that period, particularly while I was Dean; to Oxford University Press for patiently awaiting a very late manuscript; to Patricia and Bridget Pipe-Fowler for tolerating too many hours of writing snatched at anti-social times.

# Contents

# 1

# Introduction

Some of the best twentieth-century literary criticism has been that which has focused on the language of the works being discussed: William Empson's *Seven Types of Ambiguity* (1930) and the Cambridge tradition of 'practical criticism' which Empson's work and that of I. A. Richards inspired and sustained; in the United States, the 'New Criticism' of the 1940s and 1950s; in France, the earlier work of the 'Structuralists' such as that of Roland Barthes in the 1960s. The values and the terminologies employed by the critics in those movements might today be somewhat quaint, but a general principle of attentiveness to language seemed to be tacitly agreed. These critics routinely anchored their interpretative and evaluative commentaries to specific linguistic constructions within the texts: to distinctive word-orders, choices of vocabulary, patterns of sound and rhythm, complexities and idiosyncracies of meaning, and so on. One might disagree with their views on the texts, but, thanks to the fact that these critics do refer to objective structures of language, it is at least possible to query and discuss the claims being made in relation to the evidence being offered.

Informed appeal to language construction much improved the quality of debate between established academic literary critics; they became less inclined to discuss literature in terms of such qualities as their own feelings, or the author's presumed intentions, or abstract aesthetic properties, or simple moral judgements. Even more important, though, was acceptance of the lesson of language within literary *education*. At a very early stage, I. A. Richards's *Practical Criticism* (1929), though linguistically unsophisticated, firmly advocated close attention to the evidence which the text itself had to offer; and his polemical discussion of the practice of criticism was concerned directly with the impressionism and wrong-headedness he found among students reading English at Cambridge. From the end of the 1930s, a series of very influential university textbooks was published which brought home to teachers and students the need to make language the focus of literary commentary: the enormously popular *Understanding Poetry* (1938) by Cleanth Brooks and Robert Penn Warren began this tradition of textbooks encouraging the bringing of language into the centre of the literary classroom. By the time I went to university, in 1956, it was well accepted that commentary on language was a normal and essential practice within literary criticism: essential for coaxing out the complexity of literary texts, and for validating the claims one wished to make about them. These assumptions are the guiding principles for a brilliant book by a tutor of mine at University College London, Winifred Nowottny's *The Language Poets Use* (1962). Another of her pupils, David Lodge, published in 1966 a book in a similar mould, *Language of Fiction*. In the same year appeared my own *Essays on Style and Language*. I would not wish to claim that University College London had any special importance in the establishment of linguistic criticism; I cite it only to illustrate how well established these ideas were twenty-five years ago.

But a distinction must be made between two ways of studying literature 'linguistically'. On the one hand there is the activity I have just been referring to: granting priority to language and taking a good deal of notice of it. Lodge's first sentence (which surely can be applied to genres other than the novel) sums up the basic assumption: 'The novelist's medium is language: whatever he does, *qua* novelist, he does in and through language.'[1] It follows that whatever the writer 'does' can be shown by analysis of the language. But such analysis might not be attached to any particular methodology and, characteristically, critics like Lodge are methodologically eclectic and untechnical. The alternative position is methodologically much less casual. Here, the linguistic study of literary texts means, not just study of the language, but study of the language utilizing the concepts and methods of modern linguistics; the linguist M. A. K. Halliday expresses the position very clearly:

In talking therefore of the linguistic study of literary texts we mean not merely the study of the language, but rather the study of such texts by the methods of linguistics. There is a difference between *ad hoc*, personal and arbitrarily selective statements such as are sometimes offered, perhaps in support of a preformulated literary thesis, as textual or linguistic statements about literature, and a description of a text based on general linguistic theory.[2]

In fact, Halliday here implies two differences between the study of language and the linguistic study of language. First, linguistic description is technically superior because it is explicit, systematic and comprehensive. Second, the literary criticism of language is logically inferior because the critic makes up his mind in advance and then supports his claims by citing selected aspects of the text. There are problems in the way Halliday conceives of this second aspect of the comparison—it implies, falsely, that linguistic analysis is an empirical technique for discovering general properties on the basis of scrutiny of minutiae—but I will return to these problems later, in a more positive context.

The first part of Halliday's contrast is the basic claim that any linguistic critic would make: realizing, as critics do, that language is the essence of literature, and that verbal analysis is the basis of informed and plausible criticism, it makes sense to deploy the best available methods of analysis. What is best is *not* the critic's imperfect recollections of scraps of school grammar ('participle', 'past historic', 'gerund') eked out with old rhetorical terms ('zeugma', 'oxymoron') and modern value terms used pseudo-descriptively ('complex', 'cohesive', 'polyvalent'). The random descriptive jargon used by most critics who practise verbal analysis will communicate with readers only fortuitously: if, by accidents of education, critic and reader were once schooled into using the grammar term 'gerund' in a similar way; or, by brilliance of exposition, if the critic somehow succeeds in conveying to the reader just what a term like 'cohesive' means in his discourse.

A linguistic terminology has many advantages over this rather haphazard apparatus. (I am assuming that my readers have some knowledge of linguistics: this book is not meant to teach the subject from scratch.) Linguistics is an independent discipline, quite distinct, in its modern development, from literary criticism, with its own goals and criteria: this independence ensures that linguistic terms, when brought to criticism, have their own established meanings, not chameleon adaptations to the needs of the critical discourse. Students can work through a course on linguistics and emerge knowing a set of concepts which are agreed, standardized, at least within one of the major 'schools' which have theorized the subject. (There is, it must be admitted, some problem of standardization across the schools.) 'Nominalization', 'parataxis', 'paradigm', 'agent', 'morpheme', 'embedding' and so on are all stable, well-understood concepts which are readily learned and readily applied in objective description of texts.

A terminology derived from linguistics has at least two other beneficial properties, which are interconnected; it aims to be *comprehensive*; and to be *systematic*.

First, a linguistic theory aims to be *comprehensive* in offering a complete account of language structure at all levels: semantics, the organization of meanings within a language; syntax, the processes and orderings which arrange signs into the sentences of a language; phonology and phonetics, respectively the classification and ordering, and the actual pronunciation, of the sounds of speech; text-grammar, the sequencing of sentences in coherent extended discourse; and pragmatics, the conventional relationships between linguistic constructions and the users and uses of language.[3] Suppose a critic has prepared himself linguistically in all of these departments of language. Finding, say, a syntactic feature of interest in a text—perhaps an unusual word-order, an exceptional frequency of adjectives, or whatever—the critic will also be equipped to look for and account for associated features of semantic structure, let us say, or rhythm; and that ability to go from one level to others is important, because the textual features which interest critics very often embrace structure at several different levels of language.

Next, linguistic terminology is *systematic*. It is a first principle of modern linguistics, definitively formulated by the Swiss linguist Ferdinand de Saussure in 1913, that language itself is a system of units and processes (i.e. not simply a list of words and sentences). In recognition of this, the concepts denoted by descriptive linguistic terms are designed to be systematically related; for instance, the syntactic unit 'clause' is a member of the hierarchy of constituents morpheme—word—phrase—clause—sentence; noun phrases and verb phrases are related by a basic rule of the grammar S → NP + VP; prepositions are integrally related to noun phrases and only indirectly to verb phrases; and so on. The systematic nature of linguistic terminology facilitates textual description and allows it to be related readily to other texts, the language as a whole, and even Language itself.

The basic purpose of the present book, then, is to argue and to demonstrate the value to criticism of an analytic method drawn from linguistics; these claims stem from my belief that a professional linguistic analysis is better equipped for this task than an amateur commentary using only quasi-grammatical terms. (But I shall take the argument beyond this basic methodological purpose shortly.) This is a fairly brief book, and cannot provide an introduction to all of the relevant linguistic techniques; I assume that readers will be consulting other works on linguistic criticism and, even more important, will be preparing themselves independently in linguistic theory and analysis.[4] I have tried to illustrate critical analysis involving all the major levels of linguistic structure, but without attempting to cover every detail of structure within each level. Chapters 2–4 are a discussion of some fundamental semantic processes and their psychological implications. Chapter 5 gives a brief overview of linguistic structure within the sentence, and then concentrates on textual structure, particularly the various kinds of cohesive tie which link sentences together into whole texts. Chapter 6 continues with textual construction, focusing on structures which are in some sense additional to the basic linguistic requirements for well-formed texts. Chapter 7 relates texts to their real or fictional contexts of communication. Chapter 8 enters the area of interpersonal communication, examining techniques of conversational interaction as they are reproduced in plays and novels; while Chapter 9 discusses the 'orienting' devices of language, the means by which the points of view of readers and characters are constructed. Finally, Chapter 10 reverts to semantic topics: to ways in which the linguistic organization of a text suggests a particular ordering of experience.

Anyone who works through this book, and also studies a couple of the recommended linguistics textbooks, should acquire the use of a kind of linguistic toolkit: a system of concepts and terms for analysing the structure of given pieces of language (literary texts). The question remains how to employ this apparatus. Halliday condemns analysis which follows, and seeks to justify, a 'preformulated literary thesis'; so it might be thought that he is recommending the reverse procedure, namely, that linguistic analysis is first applied to the text 'cold', as it were, without prejudice or guess as to the outcome, and from this analysis emerges a critical thesis about the text. Whether or not Halliday intends to commend that sequence of argument (from analysis to thesis), it is an erroneous view both of linguistic analysis and of linguistic criticism. As Chomsky has insisted, linguistics is not a discovery procedure: not an automatic machine which, fed a text at one end, delivers at the other end some significant generalizations about the character of the text. To pursue the mechanical metaphor, it is easy to envisage a machine which would run through a text and count, say, instances of nominalizations, or abstract words, or prepositional phrases, or whatever. But that would be mechanized numerical analysis, not linguistics (which is concerned with the *nature* of nominalization as part of a speaker's knowledge); and it is certainly not criticism. A critic switching on the machine would need to have some idea that nominalization might be a significant construction and so worth counting; and s/he would need to interpret the numbers that issued as output of the analysis: interpretation which would be guided by the hunch which selected nominalization for study in the first place. This interplay between thesis and analysis is essential to criticism, and it is illustrated throughout the book. I think Chapter 10 provides some of the clearest examples. My discussion of the extract from *Melmoth the Wanderer* (pp. 158–62), for example, concentrates on constructions in which inanimate objects seem to function as agents of action verbs, or as experiencers of human feelings. The significance of these observations does not emerge directly from textual structure itself, but only from our knowledge of the relationship between the text and its literary–historical context, 'Gothic' discourse. Then, as the examples which follow *Melmoth* in Chapter 10 show, there is by no means an invariant relationship between linguistic structure and critical significance. Purely linguistic analysis cannot reveal this significance: only a critical analysis which realizes the text as a mode of discourse can do so; and treating text as *discourse* stretches the capability of linguistics as presently constituted, taking us towards a theory of language in its full, dynamic, functioning within historical, social and rhetorical contexts.

While agreeing with Halliday, then, that linguistic criticism ought to be based on concepts drawn from a proper linguistic theory—this being much more efficient and objective than the terms of conventional literary criticism—I must emphasize that linguistics *as such* is not a discovery procedure and not a critical procedure: therefore it needs to be guided by some working hypotheses which will be checked against the linguistic evidence, and progressively modified and confirmed, as the analysis proceeds. Critics who are hostile to the use of linguistics in literary criticism have sometimes misrepresented linguistics as a kind of inhuman machine capable only of soullessly dismantling literary works. This is a misleading caricature of linguistic criticism; I hope that this book will do something to reassure critics that it does not work in that mechanical way.

What then are to be the sources of the general hypotheses which are to guide the activity of linguistic criticism? To some extent, parts of the general framework can be drawn from existing literary criticism, and that is what I have done in some sections of this book; but I must insert a general caveat. It is not realistic to assume that all the general premises and values of literary criticism can be maintained intact while linguistic analysis is borrowed and incorporated as an efficient methodological aid. For a start, many of the assumptions with which literary critics work are questionable; for example, it will be evident as my book proceeds that I find fault with the assumptions which critics make about 'literature' being a special and autonomous form of discourse.[5] Second, linguistic analysis is not 'just' a neutral method of analysis compatible with any theoretical framework. A model of analysis is a model of language, that is to say, it essentially implies a theory of the nature of language in the process of describing it: such theory may be quite at odds with what is presupposed by a critical model. For example, a transformation–generative grammar (TG) is dedicated to accounting for what is *universal* in language: if a syntactic construction in a text is identified as, say, 'centre-embedded', the generative linguist's main interest is in establishing that centre-embedding is one process available within the total set of syntactic possibilities afforded by human language as a whole. TG will offer no explanation of why that structure occurs in that utterance, or what its effect is —precisely the sort of *particular* observation which criticism is interested in. A *functional* model of grammar, on the other hand, of the type employed in this book, is specifically geared to allow individual observations and explanations, so is much better suited to the task. Many other examples could be given to show that a linguistic model cannot be fitted to a critical model willy-nilly: linguistics is not a co-operative slave and will not perform tasks which are against its general principles.

When I talk about linguistic models fitting or not fitting critical models, I should not wish to give the impression that this is entirely a neat and decidable question. Schools of literary criticism are often vague and unselfcritical as far as theory and precise formulation are concerned. The linguist wishing to adopt a theoretical framework from criticism will find some ideas solid and useful, even explicit, and many unworkably mysterious and contradictory. What I have done, in order to give some shape to this book other than a catalogue of linguistic constructions, is attempt to explicate, in a helpful rather than negative way, a number of critical categories that seem to make desirable and compatible broad additions to the kind of linguistics I wish to work with. But I have not attempted to conceal tensions between linguistic and literary theory in other areas; I return to these tensions shortly.

I have felt at liberty to make extensive use of the concepts of *habitualization* and *defamiliarization*, even to incorporate them in the foundation of my whole approach (Chapters 2–4); but with a firm dissociation from the notion that these ideas constitute a theory of Art; and with a strict linking to linguistic categories. Habitualization seems to me to be based on solid principles in the psychology of meaning. Quite simply, meanings become firmly established in the minds of members of a society in so far as they are coded in conventional, often used and familiar, forms of expression. Halliday's theory of language as 'social semiotic' provides an account of how different classes of linguistic structure become imprinted with conventional meanings. Then (logically; but thirty years earlier than Halliday) Orwell's widely accepted contention that conventional word-uses render meanings stale, imprecise and automatic offers a plausible account of the degeneration of social semiotic, and seems to be a perfect linguistic version of Shklovsky's psychological theory of the staleness of over-familiar objects. I proceed to show how various critical and linguistic practices can break the conventional coding and promote defamiliarization.

A second concept found in much literary criticism (under various names) which seems to work well in linguistic terms is *cohesion*. This is the notion—a positively evaluative notion in literary studies—that literary texts are unified by linkings, echoes, and correspondences across sections larger than the sentence. There is the related idea that cross-sentence correspondences give rise to extra dimensions of meaning. I have in Chapters 5 and 6 tried to show how these cohesive processes relate to constructive principles of all language, and then applied them in analysis of 'literary' examples.

A third valuable idea which I have drawn from literary criticism is *point of view*: a difficult and rather intuitive category in literary criticism, but well established and apparently indispensable. My interest in this topic stems partly from my belief that point of view ought to be a standard part of *linguistic* theory, if linguistics manages to extend itself beyond the sentence to account for the communicative processes of whole texts. Point of view concerns all features of orientation: the position taken up by the speaker or author, that of the consciousnesses depicted in the text, and that implied for the reader or addressee. In Chapter 9 I explore these matters; and I depart somewhat from my normal mode of exposition in following quite closely the account of one writer, the literary theoretician Boris Uspensky, who stands usefully between literature and linguistics: I have attempted to render his theory more strictly linguistic. Chapter 10, 'Meaning and world-view', goes into more detail on one aspect of point of view; and returns us to the semantic topics with which the book opens. It has traditionally been suggested that consistent stylistic choices signify particular, distinctive, orderings of experience; different outlooks on the world.[6] Here I explain how this could work in fictional discourse; I relate the suggested world-views of authors and characters to different linguistic options.

In the last three paragraphs I have picked out some of the issues discussed where general literary notions and the concepts of one linguistic theory—my modification of Halliday's 'functional' linguistics—seem to correspond fairly closely, and to illuminate each other and suggest mutual development. However, the relationship between the two disciplines is generally less co-operative; a relationship of tension and critique. I must make it clear that I do not regard this as at all a bad thing, since both of the

subjects which linguistic criticism puts into juxtaposition are in
need of some degree of reform. Here I will just draw attention to
one central, crucial, controversy between the two disciplines: this
is the debate on the fundamental issue of the status and nature
of literature. I reported at the outset that much of the most
respected literary criticism this century has been that which
grounds its interpretations on objective features of the language
of texts; and I suggested that, in this context, the use of linguistic
analysis ought to be a natural development towards even greater
objectivity. But this suggestion has been vehemently rejected by
the critics; and for largely unacknowledged reasons. Careful
study of the wording of Lodge's statement quoted on p. 2 above
may be revealing. Language is a 'medium' for the novelist,
presumably analogous to paint, bronze, or celluloid. This metaphor easily comes to mean '*only* a medium': the real thing is the
novel (or poem, etc.) which is conveyed 'in and through' the
medium. Thus the substance of literature is shifted into some
obscure, undefined, sphere of existence which is somehow
beyond language. But for linguistics, literature *is* language, to be
theorized just like any other discourse; it makes no sense to
degrade the language to a mere medium, since the meanings,
themes, larger structures of a text, 'literary' or not, are uniquely
constructed by the text in its inter-relation with social and other
contexts. This position is difficult for literary critics, because it
appears to remove the claimed special status (and value) of literature, to reduce it to the level of the language of the market-place.
But this levelling is essential to linguistic criticism if the whole
range of insights about language provided by linguistics is to
be made available. We want to show that a novel or a poem is a
complexly structured text; that its structural form, by social
semiotic processes, constitutes a representation of a world, characterized by activities and states and values; that this text is
a communicative interaction between its producer and its con-
sumers, within relevant social and institutional contexts. These
characteristics of the novel or poem are no more than what functional linguistics is looking for in studying, say, conversations or
letters or official documents. Perhaps this is a richer and thus
more acceptable characterization of the aims of linguistic analysis than literary critics usually expect. But for me at any rate, this
is what theorization *as* language involves. No abstract literary

properties 'beyond' the medium need to be postulated, for the rhetorical and semiotic properties in question should appear within an ordinary linguistic characterization unless linguistics is conceived in too restricted a way.

On p. 7 above I raised the question of what might be the sources of knowledge and hypotheses for guiding linguistic analysis in the more ambitious activity of linguistic criticism. I only partially answered this by referring to literary criticism and theory as a source for *some* concepts of a quasi-theoretical kind (point of view, etc.). Other parts of the answer to this question derive from the characteristics of the linguistic model I am proposing. It should be clear by now that I do not conceive of linguistics as a mere mechanical technique for detailing the construction of texts within the narrow bounds of syntax and phonology. The key difference between my approach and, say, the classic linguistic analysis applied by Roman Jakobson to poems,[7] is that the linguistic model which I use makes a serious attempt to include *pragmatic* dimensions of language. Pragmatics is about relationships between language and its users. It is a part of linguistics which is still very much subject to debate and development, but it is clear that it includes roughly the following topics: the interpersonal and social acts that speakers perform by speaking and writing; thus, the structure not only of conversation but also of all other sorts of linguistic communication as *interaction* (see Chapter 8); the diverse relationships between language use and its different types of context (see Chapter 7); particularly the relationships with social contexts and their historical development; and, fundamentally, the systems of shared knowledge within communities, and between speakers, which make communication possible—this is where pragmatics and semantics overlap.

If linguistics is extended in this way, out into the pragmatics of communication, and incorporates a socially based semantics, then it becomes natural to refer to social structure, history, and the development of ideas as essential parts of a linguistic criticism. These are aspects of the context of literature which traditionally have *not* been attended to very much by those literary critics who have concentrated on language—indeed, the relevance of history and of social context has often been dismissed by critics; and earlier, more formalist, conceptions of linguistics may have encouraged this rejection. But it is fundamental to my approach that the significance of linguistic structures in literature is a function of the relationships between textual construction and the social, institutional, and ideological conditions of its production and reception. Thus history, social structure, and ideology are major sources of knowledge and hypotheses in the framework for linguistic criticism. Unfortunately I cannot delve into these areas in any detail for all examples analysed in this short book, but I return to the issues, with some illustrations, in my concluding chapter.

## Notes

1. David Lodge, *Language of Fiction* (London: Routledge and Kegan Paul, 1966), p. ix.
2. M. A. K. Halliday, 'The Linguistic Study of Literary Texts', in Seymour Chatman and Samuel R. Levin, eds., *Essays on the Language of Literature* (Boston: Houghton-Mifflin, 1967), pp. 217–23.
3. Note that I have defined linguistics more inclusively than is customary. The inclusion of text-grammar and pragmatics makes linguistics much more compatible with criticism than older, narrower, conceptions of the subject are.
4. A classified list of Further Reading is provided on pp. 183–6 below. This list is selective: I have recommended only those books and articles which are directly useful in relation to my approach. In addition, footnotes in each chapter refer to writings which give specific technical support for my discussion of particular topics. Readers should make a special effort to follow up those references.
5. For longer and more polemical discussions of this topic, see my *Literature as Social Discourse* (London: Batsford, 1981).
6. See, for example, Leo Spitzer, *Linguistics and Literary History* (Princeton, NJ: Princeton University Press, 1948).
7. Roman Jakobson, 'Closing Statement: Linguistics and Poetics', in T. A. Sebeok, ed., *Style in Language* (Cambridge, Mass.: MIT Press, 1960), pp. 350–77; Jakobson and Claude Lévi-Strauss, 'Charles Baudelaire's "Les Chats" ', in R. and F. DeGeorge, ed. and trans., *The Structuralists from Marx to Lévi-Strauss* (New York: Doubleday, 1972), pp. 124–46.

# 2
# Language and Experience

Literature is a creative use of language—not the only form of creativity in language, as we shall see, but certainly the one that people most immediately acknowledge as creative. What is created, and how? 'How?' is answered in this book's exploration of linguistic technique. In this chapter I begin to explain what is created, starting with some observations on the relationship between language and experience.

One aspect of literature's creativity is the production of works that seem to be 'new' in a special sense. I am not referring just to 'experimental' or 'avant-garde' works. Even traditional kinds of writing can provide the surprise of a new voice, one which seems to be quite distinct from its predecessors and from the mass of language which surrounds us in our everyday lives. This distinctiveness of phrasing, or metre, or metaphor, may be experienced even in works which are not of our time, even texts several centuries old.

But it is not just newness of *language* which we experience when we feel that a literary work is innovative—if that were the recipe for literary creativity, then verbal acrobatics of the most striking kind would guarantee literary success. Verbal tricks are not enough. The important thing that is created is new knowledge. Readers come away from a novel or a poem feeling that they have been given some knowledge which they did not possess before, or, very often, that they have experienced a new insight into some familiar problem or theme. There is a sense of absolute focus and exactness in the presentation of an idea which makes the idea itself unique. Now this is not a result of the claims or assertions that are made directly by texts: 'Beauty is truth, truth beauty'. 'The proper study of mankind is Man', 'Brevity is the soul of wit'. The new knowledge seems rather to be a consequence of the way the writer's arrangement of language analyses afresh the topic of beauty or Man or wit. For the reader, a new prospect or perspective is opened up, sometimes without his being aware how: the linguistic devices may be quite diffuse or indirect and unobvious, which is one of the justifications for the present book. As a brief example, consider this famous couplet from Pope's *Rape of the Lock*, which, while it gives no tremendously illuminating insight on the nature of life, does nevertheless make a social judgement with devastating precision:

> Not louder Shrieks to pitying Heav'n are cast,
> When Husbands or when Lap-dogs breathe their last.

Pope mockingly attacks the values of fashionable women: Belinda's anguish at the rape of the lock exceeds that of women on the death of their husbands. That distortion of values is bad enough, but worse is the equation of husbands and lapdogs, the devaluation of the former and overvaluation of the latter, the implication that husbands are regarded as lapdogs in their living as well as at their deaths. The lines do not state any of this, but the structure of the verse organizes our perception of the ideas concerned precisely, economically and uniquely.

We may say that Pope has *encoded* this complex social judgement, used language to establish it as an exact concept. The reader who decodes the language acquires it as a concept which is new to him or her. The insight remains fresh two and a half centuries later because of the extreme efficiency and compression of the language, which gives the reader the sense that he or she experiences the concept as Pope invents it and in the exact form in which he conceives it.

I want to repeat that the kind of effect which I illustrated from Pope, and which is found on a much more striking scale in other works, is not a defining characteristic of literature, nor is it encountered only in texts which our society treats as literary. The creation of new meanings and thus new knowledge is a property of all language, and it happens to be an expected and appreciated part of the texts which modern European and American societies accept as their literatures—so that verbal techniques which facilitate this kind of creativity have been extensively developed in these literatures. Before examining the way these linguistic techniques work in literature, we must return to their basic principles as they work in all language.

We must consider some quite complicated relationships between individual people, social structure, language, and the world.

Here is a rather strong, but clear statement about some of the relationships I have in mind, by the anthropologist Edmund Leach:

I postulate that the physical and social environment of a young child is perceived as a continuum. It does not contain any intrinsically separate 'things'. The child, in due course, is taught to impose upon this environment a kind of discriminating grid which serves to distinguish the world as being composed of a large number of separate things, each labelled with a name. This world is a representation of our language categories, not vice versa. Because my mother tongue is English, it seems self evident that *bushes* and *trees* are different kinds of things. I would not think this unless I had been taught that it was the case.[1]

The 'continuum' is reminiscent of the physicist's 'flux of atoms'. From other things that Leach says in this paper, it seems that he believes that the world has no intrinsic structure but receives the structure that human beings *think* it has from the influence of their language. Actually, the argument does not depend on Leach or anyone else assuming *no* structure. All we have to challenge is the common but fallacious assumption that the world has a natural structure from which language draws its meanings passively, by reflection as it were. It could well be that the world has one set of structural characteristics, is one set of 'separate things', but that language chops it up into a different set of things. The important point is to acknowledge the active role of language in providing a classification of phenomena and of our experience.

The world human beings live in is complex and potentially bewildering. It is so because our brains make us capable of experiencing it this way: we are always aware of a multitude of factors beyond any present situation in which we are living, we remember a great deal, we make many connections between and discriminations between things and events. The complexity is increased by social organization and by technological activity. We live in large, though loosely linked, social groups, often with large populations packed into small geographical spaces. The material needs of such populations can be provided for only by a complicated division of labour which generates thousands of functions from bank management to waste disposal. The consequence of living in an industrialized, urbanized society, for the individual, is that s/he is forced to be aware of great numbers of others and also to be conscious of the function of others. As for technology, this is devoted to transforming the physical (and inevitably, social) environment: to producing new objects, new functions for objects; to extending the range and power of humanity's knowledge about and control over the world. Obvious examples of the way technology increases and diversifies people's contact with the world are television and air travel, but earlier and simpler innovations would still demonstrate the same principle.

Now it is clear that this proliferation of available experience is willed by human beings, and is a product of a drive towards knowledge and discovery which motivates both the preoccupation with creativity with which I began this chapter and the co-operative ‚social organization which helps the individual achieve more than his own physical capacity would allow. (This drive has been trivialized as material acquisitiveness and useless competitiveness, in the conditions of industrial capitalism, but that is another matter.) But if the complexity of their world is a privilege for human beings, there is also the penalty that this world can be perplexing and overwhelming. The process of categorization that Leach describes is part of a general strategy for simplifying and ordering the world.

We understand the multitude of things and events we encounter in our daily lives by seeing them as instances of types or categories. This strategy allows infinite variation to be simplified, irrelevant features to be ignored. Everyone knows what a table or a weed or a pet is. When an instance of one of these categories is encountered, we assume that some central, defining feature is applicable and that other, idiosyncratic qualities are not significant: you can place a book or a cup on a table whether it has four legs or five or one; a weed should be torn up from the garden even if it sports an attractive flower; a pet may be admitted to the sitting room even if it is a cobra. The economies which follow from this categorizing attitude are very clear. For instance, if you meet someone for the first time and he is introduced to you as a lawyer, a postman, or whatever, you assume that he has had certain experiences typical of lawyers, and so quickly build up a framework of speculative ideas about him which will help you talk appropriately to him even before you know exactly what his life-history has been. If someone writes to tell you they have bought a bungalow, you don't write back asking whether it has open-tread stairs. As we shall see, the economy of types also carries dangers: the type, rather than being a provisional hypothesis allowing us to begin to understand a phenomenon, may become a stereotype which inhibits understanding; thought become routine, uncritical. Something of this kind can be detected in my sentence introducing the example of 'a lawyer' which unthinkingly assumes male sex. However, without any categorization, it is doubtful whether we could think or communicate at all—we would be overwhelmed by individual impressions, unclassifiable and therefore incomprehensible.

It seems, then, that human beings do not engage directly with the objective world, but relate to it by means of systems of classification which simplify objective phenomena, and make them manageable, economical subjects for thought and action. In a sense, human beings create the world twice over, first transforming it through technology and then reinterpreting it by projecting classifications on to it. Because classification appears to be natural, members of a community regard their assumptions and types as 'common sense'. It would be more accurate to call these attitudes 'world-view' or 'theory' or 'hypothesis' or 'ideology'. The last of these terms, 'ideology', is often used to accuse a community of holding false or distorted theories of reality. In a sense all theories are 'distortions', since they are interpretations or representations rather than reflections. If one needs to use the terms 'ideology' and 'ideological' pejoratively, it seems better to apply them to unexamined, unselfcritical, routinized presentations of the world, rather than to brand world-views as false.

So far I have suggested that people analyse the world, sort it into categories, impose structure on it, in order to avoid being overwhelmed by its richness. I have implied that this procedure is not deliberate: the widely held notion of 'common sense' suggests that people believe that their theory of the way the world works is a natural reflection of the way the world *does* work. Now it seems that a number of basic 'cognitive categories' do arise in individuals naturally and are a product of the way we are constructed biologically. These include basic colour categories, such as black and white, red and green; certain geometrical figures, such as circle, triangle, and rectangle; notions of movement, such as up, down, forward, backward; logical relationships, such as oppositeness, identity, and causation.[2] But the majority of our ideas are *not* natural. My examples 'pet', 'weed', and 'table' will illustrate this. All three concepts are, on reflection, *social* in origin. I have no doubt that there are societies which do not keep unproductive animals in the home, that is to say which divide up the world of animals into different sets than we do—'working animals' and 'animals for food', or 'working animals' and 'food animals' and 'sacred animals' (without 'pets'). Our ancestors cherished for their medicinal properties plants which we would root out as weeds. What counts as an instance of a category is subject to negotiation and revision. Can a lion count as a pet? Yes, the magistrates say, provided it is locked up securely. A recent dispute in this area concerned giant African cockroaches. Clearly the idea of 'pet' cannot be derived from any list of actual animals; it is not a natural feature of certain animals but a property of the culture's system of attitudes towards animals. The idea 'pet' is a cultural category. 'Black' and 'square' and 'upright', by contrast, are natural categories.

Returning to the ideas raised in the extract from Edmund Leach, I want to take up his suggestion that language plays a major part in establishing the systems of ideas or 'theories' which human beings impose on the world. I do not think it is true that, as Leach suggests, categorization depends necessarily and exclusively on language. Rather, language is a central part of social process and is a highly efficient medium in the coding of social categorizations. The obvious role of language is the expression of the discriminations which a culture needs to make, but its role goes further than that. Language does not just provide words for already existing concepts; it crystallizes and stabilizes ideas. As Edward Sapir said, a

concept does not attain to individual and independent life until it has found a distinctive linguistic embodiment . . . As soon as the word is at hand, we instinctively feel, with something of a sigh of relief, that the concept is ours for the handling. Not until we own the symbol do we feel that we hold a key to the immediate knowledge or understanding of the concept.

An idea encoded has a clear identity because it has material substance: it can be spoken and written. Because English has two words 'flower' and 'weed', the ideas are palpably distinct for English speakers, notwithstanding the existence of borderline cases. Words help us remember ideas and, better still, help us store them as *systems* of ideas.[3] They allow us to express distinctions and relationships: 'A square has four sides, a triangle three', 'A weed is a plant', 'Scarlet and vermilion are shades of red'; through such sentences we explore and establish the structure of our community's body of knowledge. They provide labels to attach to objects in the physical world: 'That's a tree.' Even though, as we have seen, the concept 'tree' is not a single fact of nature but a cultural unit which simplifies the facts of nature, our possessing one word 'tree' assists our belief in the singleness of the concept 'tree'. The same principle caters for abstractions: the ideas 'truth', 'beauty', 'democracy' are not tangible, but then no more is the idea 'table'. All meanings are abstractions. In the case of ideas like 'truth' or 'anger', the existence of words makes them plausible and makes them manageable: the community can use the words to convert the ideas into actions. Sapir asks, rhetorically, 'Would we be so ready to die for "liberty", to struggle for "ideals", if the words themselves were not ringing within us?'

The meanings of the words in a language are the community's store of established knowledge. A child learns the values and preoccupations of its culture largely by learning the language: language is the chief instrument of socialization, which is the process by which a person is, willy-nilly, moulded into conformity with the established systems of beliefs of the society into which s/he happens to be born. Language gives knowledge, and allows knowledge to be transmitted from person to person. But this knowledge is traditional, not innovative, for language is a stabilizing, stereotyping, mode of communication. I will return to these negative implications of the medium, and to literature as a resistance to stereotyping, in the next two chapters. In the meantime there are some more points to be made about language and the representation of experience.

Although *vocabulary* is the part of language which most obviously sorts experience into concepts and systems of concepts, other aspects of language have this effect, too. Especially, *syntax*: the arrangement of words into phrases, clauses, and sentences. Different syntactic arrangements encode different meanings even though the words may remain the same, even though the 'statement' is the same. This fact will be amply illustrated in later chapters, but here are some quick examples.

I may say 'I'm cold' or 'It's cold', and in each case I am commenting on the same sensation, my discomfort in feeling cold. In a given situation, the difference may go unnoticed both by myself and anyone I am talking to. But my syntax in the first comments directly on my own feeling, whereas the second attributes my discomfort to the world outside me. The example in itself is mundane, but suppose I use the 'it's . . .' construction consistently in cases where I *might* have used a syntax that focused on myself as an experiencer or actor: perhaps, if that happens, I am betraying myself as a person who blames 'the world' rather than facing up to my own participation in the world's processes.

Or, consider phrases like 'my wife', 'my son', 'my assistant'. Being any of these people involves activity, relationship. But the syntax which is conventional in English—Possessive + Noun— has the unfortunate effect of encoding a human relationship as an *object*, a possession of another person, so that 'my wife' seems to be as totally owned by me as my hand or my books or my car. Obviously this syntactic structure, apparently so 'natural', embodies a theory of personal relationship as ownership with dominance, with the dominated partner reduced to the status of an object. Once recognized, such processes are seen as ideological and objectionable. It is claimed that they encourage habits of mind and behaviour which are prejudicial to the dignity and the economic progress of the people presented as 'possessed'. If this is (as seems likely) true, then such examples illustrate well how active and powerful a role language plays within social process.

It will become evident as we go on that, as well as vocabulary and syntax, still further levels of linguistic structure are involved in encoding meanings—and in turn, consolidating these meanings and mobilizing them in practical action. I have in mind the 'stylistic' and 'socio-linguistic' dimensions of discourse, the conventions which communicate such features as politeness, formality, genre (novel, ode, Irish joke, official notice, legal document, etc.), membership of social, geographical and occupational groups, and so on. Many of these conventions will be discussed later on. At this stage I simply want to acknowledge their existence and importance. A great diversity of linguistic structures is involved, and to offer just a few illustrations here would be misleading.

Edmund Leach's examples, and mine too, featured everyday

words and concepts which everyone knows. I chose illustrations such as 'table' and 'pet' because I wanted to make the point that not even the most familiar ideas are 'natural', that they are in fact the result of a process of cultural coding. The ordinariness of the examples could mislead in another direction. I do not take the language and the ideas of a culture to be 'what everyone knows'. To look at the issue from another perspective: the culture and the language are fields of knowledge greater than the experience of any individual. We live in an immensely diversified society, and this fact has two linked consequences.

First, the individual is born into, and socialized into, the experience of a particular section of society; factors which bear upon his position include parents' occupation and income, his own education, whether he lives in a city or the country, what his job is, what he reads, where and how much he travels, and so on. A country like Great Britain is multiply divided in these respects. As a result, each person in his or her language encodes knowledge which is peculiar to a certain group and different from that encoded by other groups. This diversity of language and associated ideology is, on reflection, strikingly obvious when people of different generations, or geographical areas, or sexes, or occcupations, talk together. (I say 'on reflection' because there is a principle of co-operation in dialogue which works to reduce these differences.)

Second, the circumstances in which communication occurs are tremendously varied, and they bring forth very different modes of language and thought.[4] There is variation from the highly ritualized speech of a religious ceremony on the one hand to the loose and free conversation of intimates on the other. Speech and written or printed language require different syntactic organizations and choices of vocabulary. Within each of those two media, style will vary radically depending on purpose, intended audience, the authority of the source, and so on. What is appropriate for newspapers will not suit scientific textbooks. Within the Press, there are striking linguistic contrasts between papers addressed to audiences of different social groups. Scores of other contrasts in the kinds of language used in different circumstances can readily be thought up, and, although the examples themselves may be very diverse, it will emerge that similar causes are recurrently at work. Prominent among them are the status, roles, and occupations of participants, with *inequality* of status—age, money, informedness, etc.—being particularly influential; the type of communicative event (personal correspondence, interview, ceremony, school lesson); the medium (speech, writing, script for reading aloud, etc.); the channel (face-to-face, indirect, one-to-many, etc.). The persistence with which such factors recur suggests that communicative events may be systematically classified with reference to them. Linguists have not agreed on a classification, but we can at least say that language-users recognize speech situations as belonging to regular types, and that they assess the situation and produce appropriate words and appropriate responses to other people's words—within the areas of communicative competence which they have mastered, which, as we have seen, is by no means the whole of the linguistically-coded knowledge of the community.

I am now going to move from theory to illustration. I want to demonstrate how the structure of the language chosen in a particular communication creates a grid of meaning which encourages a slanted perspective[5] on what is being presented by the communication. This grid of meaning constitutes the theory or ideology of the speaker, his analysis of the communicated content according to the system of relevant beliefs he has been socialized into holding and into coding in his habitual language usage. If we hold the same beliefs, the analysis is likely to seem 'natural'; if we do not, it may strike us as tendentious or false—though ideology is often difficult to spot and therefore potentially insidious.

My example comes from the language—or languages—of the Press. The following three headlines appeared in *The Observer*, *The Sunday Times*, and *The Sunday Telegraph* on 12 December, 1976:

1. NUS regrets fury over Joseph.
2. Student leaders condemn insult to Keith Joseph.
3. Student chiefs 'regret' attack on Sir Keith.

The headlines stand above reports of a sequence of events involving the conference of the National Union of Students and Sir Keith Joseph, a prominent right-wing member of the Conservative opposition party in Parliament. On Friday, 10 December, Keith Joseph had attempted to attend the conference as an observer, was spotted, abused, and asked to leave after a voted decision by the delegates that he should not be allowed to stay. All but two members of the NUS executive had voted for his expulsion. The next day, the executive issued a rather tongue-in-cheek statement which might be taken to hint an apology to Keith Joseph. The newspaper reports give a brief account of the scene at the conference, and more space to the Saturday statement and to comments by various protagonists and interested parties.

On superficial examination, these three sentences all seem to say the same thing. Yet they have noticeably different tonal connotations—which are consistent with the political 'lines' taken by the three newspapers—and on close scrutiny appear ultimately to offer different analyses of the 'reality' they report.

The different ways in which the participants are named are significant: naming conventions are extremely regular and revealing in English. The *Observer*'s 'Joseph' suggests formality and distance; the *Sunday Telegraph*'s 'Sir' connotes respect while the first name 'Keith' suggests intimacy. The connotations agree exactly with the papers' political characters: the *Observer* claims to be liberal and is not likely to be in sympathy with Keith Joseph; the *Sunday Telegraph* is a right-wing paper likely to admire such a politician. *The Sunday Times*'s 'Keith Joseph' seems to be neutral and non-committal. The *Observer*'s 'NUS' makes it plain that the paper recognizes the National Union of Students as a legitimate organization well enough known to its readership to be identified by initials. 'Student leaders' and 'student chiefs'—the latter with its implications of savagery or thuggery—are less sympathetic. The syntax of 'student leaders' could mean 'people who lead students' or 'people who are studying to be leaders' or 'students who lead students': the equivocation tends to undermine the status of the people referred to. Also 'student leaders', like 'student chiefs', evokes a range of comparable belittling phrases: 'petty tyrant', 'student nurse', 'junior officer', 'boy king', 'learner driver', etc.

These are fairly obvious observations which require very little linguistics for their demonstration. But the fact is that we *do* respond to features such as these; that the connotations are not random—they arise from systematic conventions in the way the British handle their language; that, if we were not faced with the comparison, we would absorb the suggestions of the version chosen by our newspaper without noticing the process of bias.

There are more powerful and more insidious differences. The words 'regrets', 'condemn', and ' "regret" ' are subtle variants which carry major distinctions of meaning. Though both 'regret' and 'condemn' mean basically 'judge adversely', they differ in a number of important ways. 'Condemn' is an act, albeit an act of speech: 'state condemnation of'. *The Sunday Times*'s 'condemn' merely reports that the NUS issued a statement condemning the insult to Keith Joseph: it does not commit itself one way or the other on the sincerity of the statement. 'Regret', on the other hand, is *either* an act of speech *or* a mental state: 'state regret' or 'feel regret'. In principle, the *Observer*'s 'NUS regrets' is ambiguous: either the paper is reporting that the NUS issued a statement of regret, or it is reporting that the NUS experienced a feeling of regret. In the latter case, the *Observer* would probably commit itself to accepting the NUS's sincerity: certainly the phrasing allows the reader to assume that the *Observer* believes in the NUS's sincerity. The *Sunday Telegraph* leaves us in no doubt. By putting ' "regrets" ' in quotation marks, the paper declares that it is merely reporting an act of speech, and implicitly casts doubt on the sincerity of that act: 'they say that they regret, but we don't believe they really regret.' Another difference between 'condemn' and 'regret' is that the former is transitive and the latter reflexive: one condemns somebody else's actions, but regrets one's own—or at least, one regrets the actions of someone for whom one is responsible: a parent's child, a manager's team, a union executive's membership. The distinction is crucial in relation to the words 'fury', 'insult', and 'attack', because the truncated syntax does not specify *who* was furious, *who* insulted, *who* attacked. We supply the missing subjects on the basis of what is suggested by 'condemn' and 'regret'. *The Sunday Times* suggests that it was someone other than the 'student leaders' who 'insulted Keith Joseph' whereas the *Observer* implies that it was the NUS that was furious, the *Sunday Telegraph* that the 'student chiefs' made the attack.

Finally, note that the preposition 'over' contrasts with both 'to' and 'on': these leave no doubt that Keith Joseph was the object of the insult/attack, whereas 'over' allows him other qossible roles, including, principally, the role of the person *responsible for* the NUS's fury. If one goes by the left-to-right order of words, in all three headlines the NUS is the agent of the action, Keith Joseph the object or patient: superficially, it appears from all three that the NUS did something to Keith Joseph, simply because, in English, the noun at the left of the sentence is assumed to be subject and the one on the right object. In 2 and 3, this assignment of responsibilities is reinforced by the objective prepositions 'to' and 'on'; in 1, however, the preposition 'over' suggests a subversive counter-statement 'Joseph made NUS furious':

Subject ⟶ *regrets fury over* ⟶ Object    (2 & 3)
*NUS*                                                                  *Joseph*
Object ⟵ *fury (cause)* ⟵ Subject    (1)

I am suggesting that, to put it informally, the *Observer* manages to have it both ways: simultaneously implying the NUS's responsibility in this train of events and justifying the NUS's action by putting the ultimate blame on Keith Joseph. On the other hand, *The Sunday Times* and the *Sunday Telegraph* analyse the facts in a less equivocal way: Keith Joseph is assigned the role of 'patient' in both cases, and there is no hint that he plays any more active role.

One might say that these headlines differ in 'tone', and that the differences stem from relatively minor details of the language, such as the pejorative 'chiefs' and the dissociating quotes around ' "regret" '. It is certainly the case that they differ in that way; moreover, the tones achieved are entirely consistent with the different ideologies of the papers concerned—for the *Observer* the NUS is an unexceptionable fact of life, for the *Sunday Telegraph* organized students are a problem and perhaps a threat. Loyal readers absorb these stylistic overtones, and these ideologies, without noticing them. Questions of the tone and attitude are important enough for critical comment, but in fact there is an even more serious consequence of linguistic structure in the headlines. Closer scrutiny has revealed that they differ considerably in the ways they present the basic structure of the event that is being reported. By subtle means, they convey quite distinct pictures of who did what to whom: they make different attributions of responsibility in analysing the conflict between the NUS and Keith Joseph. The structures of perception are slanted differently in the three versions. For the majority of the readership, the newspapers provide their only access to the event itself, and so the structure of the event is determined for the readers by the organization of the language. This is to say, in effect, that, whilst the events involving Keith Joseph and the NUS did actually happen in reality on 10–11 December 1976, the language in which they are presented works, for the reader, in an essentially *constitutive* (rather than merely 'reflective') fashion. The headlines 'package' the events in three different ways, so that the form of the events, and their evaluation, are perceived by each newspaper and its readers according to the way the language structure analyses them.

The constructive mode of the newspaper headlines is not essentially different from the 'creativity' of the extract from Pope, and both are extensions of the principle of coding which were examined in such simpler cases as 'bush' and 'weed'. To be critical of our own terminology for a moment, perhaps we load too great a responsibility upon literature by demanding that it should be 'creative' if what is encoded in 'creative' is no more than an ordinary capacity of language.

## Notes

1. 'Animal Categories and Verbal Abuse', in E. H. Lenneberg, ed., *New Directions in the Study of Language* (Cambridge, Mass.: MIT Press, 1964), p. 34.
2. For a good introduction to natural cognitive categories, see H. H. Clark and E. V. Clark, *Psychology and Language* (New York: Harcourt Brace Jovanovich, 1977), Ch. 14.
3. For a linguistic account of the systematicity of semantic structure, see J. Lyons, *Introduction to Theoretical Linguistics* (London: Cambridge University Press, 1968), Chs. 9 and 10, or for more detail, the same author's *Semantics*, Vol. I (Cambridge: Cambridge University Press, 1977), Chs. 8 and 9.
4. For socio-linguistic varieties, see D. Crystal and D. Davy, *Investigating English Style* (London: Longmans, 1969); P. Trudgill, *Sociolinguistics* (Harmondsworth: Penguin, 1974); J. B. Pride and J. Holmes, eds., *Sociolinguistics: Selected Readings* (Harmondsworth: Penguin, 1972). But for a more powerful statement of the relations between language, social structure and thought, see M. A. K. Halliday, *Language as Social Semiotic* (London: Edward Arnold, 1978).
5. I do not mean, necessarily, a *false* perspective, merely a perspective from a specific angle.

# 3
# Language and Criticism

Linguistic codes do not reflect reality neutrally; they interpret, organize, and classify the subjects of discourse. They embody theories of how the world is arranged: world-views or ideologies. For the individual, these theories are useful and reassuring, making his relationship with the world simple and manageable.

Since language is not just internal and passive knowledge, but activity carried out in extensive speaking, listening, writing and reading, every day, the sets of ideas encoded in language are constantly affirmed and checked. Linguistic knowledge is not just ideas, but practical knowledge of the most important kind.

It seems natural to think of language-use as a personal activity, and indeed most linguistic textbooks present linguistic interaction in terms of talk between individuals, Speaker A and Speaker B, or Jack and Jill. Similarly, linguistic knowledge is regarded as a property of an individual person, for instance Chomsky's 'ideal speaker–hearer'. Individuals do of course know and use language, but they have remarkably little freedom to invent or change meanings, or to break away from established patterns of discourse. Their language is social and conventional both in its origin and in the rules which govern the practices of speaking and writing. Language is a social practice which is manifested, or realized, in the actions of individuals. (In the production of public media such as newspapers and official reports, traces of the individual's participation may be removed.)

A convention is something shared by people. If you say that John's behaviour is conventional, you are not saying that it is consistent with itself, with his own past behaviour, but that it matches (some) other people's behaviour; perhaps, the behaviour of the majority of the population. A convention is also something relatively stable. In the case of language and other communication systems, obviously we can only communicate with one another if we assume that the meanings of signs do not vary substantially from person to person and from day to day.

This need for semantic stability is also vital in the individual's conceptual relationship with the world, as argued in the previous chapter. The conventional—if illusory—solidity of the concepts carried by language stabilizes a person's 'discriminating grid' which enables him to experience the world as an ordered, and not anarchic or random, context for living.

In ordinary usage, the word 'conventional' also has strong overtones of 'old-fashioned', 'unadventurous', 'conformist'. Since the notion of convention means basically no more than communally shared knowledge or behaviour, the secondary meaning of 'conservatism' is an interesting development. It indicates what seems to be an inevitable by-product of the useful stability I mentioned: the price paid for stability is conformism and resistance to change.

In any abstract, theoretical discussion—for example, science, politics—a writer who intends to develop any innovative ideas finds himself with a major problem of terminology, and, therefore, according to the theory I am developing in this book, a major intellectual and communicative problem. Such a writer needs to speak about existing subjects without being fettered by the language in which they are already encoded; he wants to reorient people's thoughts on these subjects, but is continually dragged back towards stock assumptions and classifications to the extent that he uses existing terminology. I can give a personal and immediate example. This book could be described as an introduction to 'linguistic structures in literature', and my readers would understand that the term 'literature' refers to a collection of texts including *King Lear, Ode to a Grecian Urn, Sons and Lovers, Jude the Obscure, The Waste Land, Beowulf*, etc. I must use the term 'literature' in this book in order to connect my discussion with my readers' experience. However, I need to use this word with extreme caution, because I reject what many of my readers would take for granted: I do not accept that all the texts called 'literature' have the same essential distinctive properties. There are similar problems, in this text of mine, with a whole range of related terms, e.g. 'art', 'value', 'significance', 'culture', 'interpretation', 'criticism', 'creative'. Existing discussions of linguistic structures in literature are dependent on that vocabulary; if I avoid it altogether, my book will be misunderstood or rejected, but I can only use the vocabulary if I carefully dissociate myself from its conventional meanings.

The difficulty is partly overcome by avoidance of tendentious terms: for example, I hardly use the word 'art' and then only to cite other people's opinions; and I try to avoid 'literary text', preferring the more neutral 'text'. Partly by defining terms: for 'text' see Chapter 5. Partly by using a new vocabulary: 'ideational', 'code', 'socio-linguistic', 'transformation', etc. These essential new terms introduce another problem, though. One way a reader might respond would be to claim that he does not understand them, despite the fact that I explain them. Another hostile reaction which I anticipate is the accusation that the terms I use are inappropriate to the subject. A very good example of this response is the wholesale rejection by Anglo-Saxon critics of all the new descriptive terminology invented by French structuralist students of literature, or the resistance of literary critics to terms drawn from social and political science.

The notion of appropriateness can be linked to the notion of common sense or ideology mentioned in the previous chapter. Conventional codes such as (indeed, primarily) language encode world-views which are accepted as common sense. This common sense is not natural, but a product of social convention. Distinguishing bushes and trees by giving them different names is not unlike distinguishing spoons and knives by using them differently at the meal-table: both distinctions are social fictions.

Common sense—the sum of the meanings of codes—is very comforting, and it is indispensable to sanity and to working communication. I want now to discuss the negative side of this distinctively human use of codes and meanings, so as to clear the way for justifying *criticism* and *creative practice* (and their relationships). The twin problems with codes and their conventional meanings are the problem of *legitimation* and the problem of *habitualization*.

To take *legitimation* first. Remember that the meanings which an individual has available were not invented by him, but were already encoded in the language he acquired as a child. It is the language of his society, not his own individual code, which he speaks and through the medium of which he sees the world. This language is an 'official' language in the sense that it comprises the structures and the meanings authorized by the dominant interests of the culture. Significantly, infants learn their language first from parents; in effect, from people who are a generation older than they are, and in absolute authority over them. They are exposed to meanings which serve the interests of an older, authoritarian group (*from the perspective of the child*, this is true even if the parents are young and poor). Education carries this process of initiation into the codes of authority further: schools and their staff are authorized by the State, and the codes of behaviour, and associated meanings, that they convey, are directly legitimated by State authority (by means of regular inspection, public examinations, compulsory teacher training at recognized institutions, etc.). The textbooks children have to work with, and the books that are available or allowed in public libraries, are 'standard' texts, approved and usually 'well-tried', published by respected, large, and commercially successful publishing houses. As children grow up, they are exposed to an official language of legitimated meanings in newspapers, films, and TV, all of these media the products of vastly powerful business and state enterprises. The dominance of legitimated language continues throughout our life. 'Real' language is that of school, book, radio, newspaper, and government. Our private language is minimal and mundane and, in so far as it discourses on social, personal, and political topics, it is deeply ideological because of its dependence on legitimated concepts.

From this source come concepts such as 'race', 'equality', 'progress', 'value', 'individual', 'love', 'intelligence', 'communication', 'work', 'law', 'authority', 'property', all the general terms which are essential to our thinking about our selves and our relationships. Writers like George Orwell and Stuart Chase have pointed out the dangers of such terms. They may encourage us to believe in spurious entities—that is a predictable development from the general principle that coded concepts are not natural but conventionally constructed. The danger really is not that such concepts are fictitious (they are after all *necessarily* so) but that they are loaded in favour of the political and economic interests that legitimate them. In our present society, this means the advantage of the holders of political office, the owners and managers of companies, and functionaries such as professors, priests, doctors, judges. It is easy to see that ideas such as 'God', 'sin', 'property', 'duty' are advantageous to some classes of people and damaging to others. If I had space, I could show how apparently innocuous and positive terms—'freedom', 'responsibility', 'independence', 'progress'—are also prejudicial. But the general point should be clear. Meaning in language is not natural but conventional. Linguists say that the coding of meanings is arbitrary, by which they mean that any sounds or letters could be used to represent any concept. But what concepts come to be represented is not an arbitrary or accidental matter. Over long periods in the history of a society, a vocabulary and phrasings develop to suit the needs of the society—those 'needs' being the interests of dominant, privileged, groups. These dominant groups control the means of legitimating the preferred systems of meanings—schools, libraries, the media. Language thus becomes a part of social practice, a tool for preserving the prevailing order. It does this not only through propaganda, but also by inertia, the settlement towards stability and resistance to change which, as I said earlier, is a characteristic of codes.

I mentioned *habitualization* as a second major problem in conventional coding. Codes simplify knowledge and behaviour by allowing particulars to be recognized as instances of a category. Take traffic signals. When we approach a red light, we stop and wait. We don't *examine* the signal. Variations in the height of signs, intensity of lights, and so on, go unnoticed. We assume that all other road-users understand and respond appropriately to the signs, so we don't pay much attention to road conditions either. If the light is green we go straight through with hardly a glance to right and left. That is, we recognize the meaning of the signal, and obey it, without looking at its context and its specific characteristics. This usually works reasonably well until something goes wrong with the lights (one sticks on red, the intersecting road stays on green), or the conventions change (you can turn right on a red light in some but not all American states), or we come across a driver who reads the conventions differently. In these exceptional circumstances we are forced to start *seeing*, rather than just *recognizing*. It becomes obvious very quickly how little we see normally. The traffic code has allowed our behaviour to become habitualized, our perception to become automatic and unanalytic. In this example, the literal dangers of habitualization are apparent.

Habitualization in language-use brings analogous hazards. The American linguist B. L. Whorf gave some examples which have become famous.[1] Working as a fire insurance risk assessor, he noticed that people's behaviour towards things correlated dangerously with what they called them. Drums which had contained petrol were referred to as 'empty drums' and were regarded as empty drums: people did not hesitate to smoke near them, ignoring the fact that volatile petrol vapour still lingered in them. A half-covered pool into which waste from a tannery was discharged was called, innocently, a 'pool of water'—it also, of course, was highly explosive because of the gases given off by decomposing animal matter. The label 'water', like 'empty', suggested quite falsely a state of affairs incompatible with combustion. Such observations impelled Whorf to research into the coding of meanings in European and American–Indian languages as a result of which he claimed that one's habitual thought and behaviour are dependent on what language one speaks:

We dissect nature along lines laid down by our native languages . . . We cut nature up, organize it into concepts, and ascribe significances as we do, largely because we are parties to an agreement to organize it in this way—an agreement that holds through our speech community and is codified in the patterns of our language. The agreement is, of course, an implicit and unstated one, but *its terms are absolutely obligatory*; we cannot talk at all except by subscribing to the organization and classification of data which the agreement decrees.

Whorf's claim that language determines the categories of thought can be accepted so long as we qualify the argument somewhat: the semantic categories are not simply properties of the language, but products of the society in which the language is moulded.

This is in fact the chain of reasoning set out by Orwell in his very emotive but essential essay 'Politics and the English Language':[2] the 'decadence' of our society encourages us to have 'foolish thoughts'; the English language 'becomes ugly and inaccurate because our thoughts are foolish, but the slovenliness of our language makes it easier for us to have foolish thoughts'. Although Orwell suggested that dishonest political language is used with conscious intent to deceive, his frequent references to 'slovenliness', 'stale phrases', 'mechanical repetition' confirm that he has in mind a process of habitualization, automatic production of pre-formed words and phrases leading to a language-use which is at best unthinking and imprecise and at worst a 'catalogue of swindles and perversions'. Orwell gives a dramatic picture of the individual using language in an absolutely habitualized mode:

When one watches some tired hack on the platform mechanically repeating the familiar phrases—bestial atrocities, iron heel, bloodstained tyranny, free peoples of the world, stand shoulder to shoulder—one often has a curious feeling that one is not watching a live human being but some kind of dummy: a feeling which suddenly becomes stronger at moments when the light catches the speaker's spectacles and turns them into blank discs which seem to have no eyes behind them. And this is not altogether fanciful. A speaker who uses that kind of phraseology has gone some distance towards turning himself into a machine. The appropriate noises are coming out of his larynx, but his brain is not involved as it would be if he were choosing his words for himself. If the speech he is making is one that he is accustomed to make over and over again, he may be almost unconscious of what he is saying, as one is when one utters the responses in church. And this reduced state of consciousness, if not indispensable, is at any rate favourable to political conformity.

This unawareness of the relationship between word and meaning leads, in Orwell's view, to an acceptance of political language which is cynically dishonest:

In our time, political speech and writing are largely the defence of the indefensible. Things like the continuance of British rule in India, the Russian purges and deportations, the dropping of the atom bombs on Japan, can indeed be defended, but only by arguments which are too brutal for most people to face, and which do not square with the professed aims of political parties. Thus political language has to consist largely of euphemism, question-begging and sheer cloudy vagueness. Defenceless villages are bombarded from the air, the inhabitants driven out into the countryside, the cattle machine-gunned, the huts set on fire with incendiary bullets: this is called 'pacification'. Millions of peasants are robbed of their farms and sent trudging along the roads with no more than they can carry: this is called 'transfer of population' or 'rectification of frontiers'. People are imprisoned for years without trial, or shot in the back of the neck or sent to die of scurvy in Arctic lumber camps: this is called 'elimination of unreliable elements'. Such phraseology is needed if one wants to name things without calling up mental pictures of them.

What I am suggesting is that all language, not just political uses, constantly drifts towards the affirmation of fixed, and usually prejudicial, categories. Criticism, and literature itself, have roles in combating this tendency.

The conditions I have described, all too briefly, create a need for a critical activity associated with the use of language in society. In summary: though language creates knowledge, aids thought and simplifies perception, this gift has two drawbacks: the categories encoded in language may become fossilized and unconscious; and they may be the products and the tools of a repressive and inequitable society. The task of linguistic criticism is to make as many language-users as possible aware of, and resistant to, these conditions. That sounds negative: and indeed 'criticism' is often regarded as a debunking activity, exposing works and writings as sham and denouncing them. Writers have long complained about the fault-finding of 'carping critics', and there is an image of the critic as totally unconstructive and pettily envious. (Many reviewers in newspapers and magazines seem to be really like this.) But the basic motivation for practising criticism is *not* negativity but a healthily sceptical inquisitiveness. The critic is interested in the conditions of, and the restrictions on, knowledge in his society; in the ways that meanings come about; in the implications of systems of meanings for members of his society; and, therefore, in the relativity and potential creativity of his *own* knowledge.[3]

Criticism is not just judgement, the claim that some work is good or bad. However, the serious critic knows that questions of value are involved—moral and social questions—in so far as the works and meanings he explores have emerged from the interplay of individual and society.

Criticism may engage with any of the products of a society which have meaning and which play a role within the processes or practices by which the society is regulated. This excludes almost no topic one could think of! We are familiar with criticism of books, plays, films, paintings, architecture, and other 'art forms'. Once it is understood that criticism is not exclusively concerned with making judgements on 'aesthetic values', then extending the idea and practice of criticism to objects and activities other than 'works of art' becomes natural. The writings of the French semiotician, Roland Barthes, illustrate this extension admirably.[4] He sees society as a network of codes speaking through all kinds of media, and he interprets and comments upon the significance of cultural objects articulated in the codes: on the meanings of fashions in clothing, cars, popular entertainment, restaurant food, wrestling, strip-tease, and so on. The moral of his analyses is that even the most commonplace objects and activities have, besides their practical functions, symbolic meanings. In fact, the cultural meanings are arguably more important than the practical purposes of objects. We tend to rationalize our possessions and actions in terms of their usefulness, and so do not perceive their primarily symbolic values. Who needs (say) an electric carving knife? It will not do anything that an ordinary knife cannot do. 'Perfect for cutting light sponge cakes—no downward pressure is needed, so you don't crush the cake.' But here the value is to draw attention to the excellence of the cake; the cutting of the cake could be performed by other instruments. Civilized man needs an electric carving knife to demonstrate his control over nature, carrying the technology of cooking and eating to an extreme and highly conspicuous level. Man (The Male) needs an electric carving knife to enhance his potency and skill with tools as he dismembers the Sunday chicken, ritually manifesting his mechanized triumph over the lower animals and his wife. He needs a wife to give him an electric carving knife for Christmas and to roast the animal which he carves on ritual occasions.

This sort of criticism may at first be dismissed as frivolous, but its seriousness and plausibility increase as analysis penetrates into the *systems* of meanings which constitute a culture. Anthropologists have shown that the conventions and technology of cooking and eating, and the exchange of women, are extremely significant social practices. The electric carving knife is an absurd object, but the example is far from trivial. Cultural criticism displays the absurdity of the object (by defamiliarizing it) and the seriousness of the meanings it expresses. The object is one expression of a part of an entire system of unconscious ideas by which human beings in western industrialized societies arrange their relationships with nature (farming, cooking) and with one another (marriage, the family). Criticism dehabitualizes our perception of the object by pointing out that it is *not* 'just a knife' but an artificial expression of an artificial meaning—which has been legitimated and commercially exploited.

Returning to linguistic symbolization and linguistic criticism, we can now define the role of the latter. Criticism is conscious analysis of the relationship between the signs—words, phrases, etc.—people produce and the meanings they communicate. Analysis of this relationship is necessarily an exploration of the social origins of meanings and the social purposes of spoken and written language. Criticism is not a self-justifying or self-contained pursuit, nor is it disinterested. It is a form of social *practice*. I try to teach my students how to practise criticism so that they become better equipped to resist habitualization and to question the structure of the society which benefits from its members' lack of critical consciousness. This practice is also *reflexive*: in so far as the critic is a member of the society whose codes he criticizes, he uses those same codes, and his analysis of them is a critical reflection on his own habits of perception and communication.

(For most of my colleagues in literature departments in universities, 'teaching criticism' means quite the opposite: it means imparting a set of received opinions about a stock of approved authors; and implicitly or (less often) explicitly teaching a standardized jargon best adapted to expressing those opinions in the form of appreciations of the approved works.)

Linguistic criticism may be practised on any use of language. It neither needs nor offers any special definition of 'literature'. In fact, there are two areas of linguistic usage which are priorities for critical analysis and which would normally be regarded as definitely non-literary. One is public, official, language: the statements of governments, administrators, legal officials, business organizations, purveyors of news, as expressed in communiqués, contracts, company reports, newspapers, etc. Such texts merit critical scrutiny because of their official origins, their direct role in shaping attitudes and meanings within a community, and the passive way in which ordinary people necessarily consume them—there is no channel through which a person can respond directly to the driving licence reminder or daily newspaper which comes through his letter box. The second area is personal discourse, talk formal and informal among individuals. What we say to other people, and how we say it, needs to be subjected to critical reflection because personal discourse so easily becomes unconscious and habitualized and because it is no freer of ideology than public language. The particular aim of linguistic criticism in the first case is demystification, demonstration of the practices by which language is used to present partial and slanted concepts as if they were innocent and natural. In the second, criticism aims at self-examination, and alertness to the permeation of our own discourse by social values which we might, on reflection, wish to eradicate or resist. In another book, three colleagues and I have analysed in detail some examples of real language in these two categories, and discussed the implications of the processes which we uncovered.[5] The 'non-literary' analyses performed in that book may be seen as both continuous with and complementary to the discussions of literary texts in the present book.

In the following chapter I will consider a set of literary styles, and an aesthetic theory, which claim that literature is itself a technique of criticism: literary texts use deliberate devices for defamiliarization. I will argue that defamiliarizing techniques are simply an extreme case of techniques of language which are available to all practitioners of language and which are found outside overtly experimental or shocking texts. I will also show that defamiliarization, though initially startling or amusing, and perhaps revelatory, is itself subject to convention and habit. Thus literary styles, becoming stale, regularly create a need for revolution and replacement (hence the peculiarly important positions of writers like Milton, Wordsworth, and T. S. Eliot), and the revision of conventions; the obscuring of old conventions in the mists of history justifies an activity of critical interpretation to keep the best of them alive and significant for contemporary readers.

## Notes

1. B. L. Whorf, ed. J. B. Carroll, *Language, Thought and Reality* (Cambridge, Mass.: MIT Press, 1956).
2. 'Politics and the English Language' [1946] in Sonia Orwell and Ian Angus, eds., *The Collected Essays, Journalism and Letters of George Orwell*, Vol. 4 (Harmondsworth: Penguin, 1970), 156–70.
3. I have found the introduction and texts in P. Connerton, ed., *Critical Sociology* (Harmondsworth: Penguin, 1976) very helpful in arriving at this definition of criticism.
4. Semiotics or semiology is the theory and description of the meanings and uses of signs, both linguistic and non-linguistic, within human society. Its founder was the Swiss linguist Ferdinand de Saussure,

whose ideas are expounded and developed in Barthes's *Elements of Semiology*, trans. A. Lavers and C. Smith (London: Jonathan Cape, 1967). See also his popular book *Mythologies*, trans. A. Lavers (London: Jonathan Cape, 1972) for illustrative analyses. A large but readable and stimulating textbook on the subject is Umberto Eco, *A Theory of Semiotics* (London: Macmillan, 1977).

5. Roger Fowler, Robert Hodge, Gunther Kress and Anthony Trew, *Language and Control* (London: Routledge and Kegan Paul, 1979).

# 4
# Linguistic Practice

Language is one of the most important areas of knowledge that human beings possess, since, as we have seen, it is a powerful influence on the way people perceive and adjust to the world outside them. This knowledge has positive and negative aspects: 'Language is not only a key. It can also be a fetter,' wrote Sapir.

Language is not just knowledge; it is also a skill, a *practice*. The practical workings of language can be seen in face-to-face conversation: people talking to one another are performing real actions through speech (asking questions, giving commands, asserting claims of truth, etc.), they are affirming and negotiating status and relationship. Even the basic process of passing meanings from one brain to another is not just an automatic, untroubled channelling of information from A to B, but a process of determining and agreeing upon meanings. Although our common code provides you and me with the core meanings of the words 'food', 'beauty', 'progress', our life experiences have been different, so we have to establish by implicit negotiation what each of us intends when a word is used, and to what extent our usages are divergent or compatible.

The linguistic activities which are visible in communication between individuals reproduce processes occurring at levels of broader social organization. Institutional utterances such as advertising, news reporting, government statements, company reports, and the like are obviously linguistic acts. They are practices which intervene in social and economic organization and regulate the positions and privileges of individuals and social groups.

The usual tendency of these practices (both personal and institutional) is towards stability, consolidation of socially legitimated areas of knowledge, modes of control and types of relationships. The processes tend to stabilize codes and habitualize perception; thought is guided along existing ruts. I have pointed out the detrimental consequences of this situation in the previous chapter. The question now to be asked is whether there are linguistic practices which resist these tendencies: activities in language which promote exploration, consciousness, change, and creativity rather than stagnation and repression. The fact that there are creative linguistic practices is my motive for writing this book, and at this point the argument can take an optimistic turn.

From my point of view, any activity is creative which is capable, under the right conditions of production and reception, of reanalysing people's theory of the way the world works. It is a precondition for this kind of creativity that whoever initiates it should expose the artificiality of a prior analysis that is being superseded. Often this questioning of existing conventions is the basic creative act that is being performed: some ideology is convincingly shown to be fallacious or at least problematic. In this case the creative thinker is operating like the critic, revealing a problem which he declines to solve, demystifying perception without offering the potentially illusory closure of a replacement theory. In linguistic terms, the processes involve *un*coding— disestablishing the received tie between a sign and a cultural unit—and optionally *re*coding—tying a newly invented concept to a sign and so establishing its validity. The ultimate process in linguistic creativity is the formation of a whole new code, a system of new linguistic arrangements encoding a whole new area of knowledge.

These effects can be produced by the use of a vast range of very diverse linguistic techniques: metaphor, clashes of style, parody, breaking of syntactic rules, invention of new words, etc. They may be found in texts of widely differing cultural status, from scientific articles to jokes to newspapers to political speeches. Creativity in language is not limited to 'literary' texts. However, 'art' (including 'literature') has, in the modern period, been given a privileged role in combating the dulling familiarity of conventional codes. The theory of habitualization and defamiliarization has been placed at the centre of their justification of art by many of art's apologists, and in the verbal, visual, and musical arts pronounced techniques of defamiliarization have been developed by such technical innovators as Apollinaire, Magritte, and Schönberg. Here is a very famous defence of art in these terms by the Russian critic Victor Shklovsky:

If we start to examine the general laws of perception, we see that as perception becomes habitual, it becomes automatic . . .

We apprehend objects only as shapes with imprecise extensions; we do not see them in their entirety but rather recognize them by their main characteristic. We see the object as though it were enveloped in a sack. We know what it is by its configuration, but we see only its silhouette. The object, perceived thus in the manner of prose perception, fades and does not leave even a first impression; ultimately even the essence of what it was is forgotten . . .

And so life is reckoned as nothing. Habitualization devours works, clothes, furniture, one's wife, and the fear of war . . . And art exists that one may recover the sensation of life; it exists to make one feel things, to make the stone *stony*. The purpose of art is to impart the sensation of things as they are perceived and not as they are known. The technique of art is to make objects 'unfamiliar', to make forms difficult, to increase the difficulty and length of perception because the process of perception is an aesthetic end in itself and must be prolonged. *Art is a way of experiencing the artfulness of an object; the object is not important* [Shklovsky's emphasis].[1]

I must say straight away that I disagree with some of these assertions—particularly the notion of 'an aesthetic end in itself' and the associated dismissal of 'the object' as 'not important'. These claims are part of an aestheticism and formalism in Shklovsky's thought, a refusal to allow literary works any connection with social and historical process for which Shklovsky has been attacked by Trotsky among others. However, it is clear that Shklovsky's defence of 'art' is founded on a conception of the psychology (though not the sociology) of knowledge and perception very similar to the one I have sketched. I have acknowledged this affinity by adopting his term 'habitualization'. In what follows I must rephrase Shklovsky's theory in terms which will be compatible with my own ideas; I believe this is fair since the foundation is the same, even if my aims and my social theory differ sharply from Shklovsky's.

Art, for Shklovsky, is characterized by the use of a range of *techniques* which promote *defamiliarization* (Russian *ostraneniye*, 'making strange'). When we speak or listen or write or read according to the normal lazy conventions of communication—his 'prose perception'—symbols are transparent, automatic, simplified. Accepting as natural a coding which is in fact arbitrary, we become acquiescent, uncritical, we acknowledge meanings without examining them. Similarly we recognize our friends without really seeing them. Defamiliarization is the use of some strategy to force us to look, to be critical. If the husband emerges from the bathroom one morning without his beard, the wife is provoked to enquire: is that the same man, is it still the category 'my husband'? This is a nice question. The 'sensible' answer (common sense, ideology) is 'of course it is; it's just John without his beard', and the 'sensible' action is to accustom herself to his new appearance so that he quickly becomes the same man. But *is* the man who transformed himself with the razor the same man? After all, he has performed the action of transforming himself. A successful technique of defamiliarization would keep that doubting question alive for as long as possible, to resist the wife's sensible re-habitualization of John as 'the same man', 'my husband'.

The basic principle of linguistic defamiliarization is well captured by Boris Tomashevsky: 'The old and habitual must be spoken of as if it were new and unusual. One must speak of the ordinary as if it were unfamiliar.'[2] There are innumerable linguistic techniques for achieving this unsettling of the relationship between a sign and its concept, this questioning of the naturalness of a coded concept. A pointedly naïve perspective can be created by withholding the usual term for something that is being described, pretending that the thing is *not* coded. One of Shklovsky's examples, from Tolstoy, describes the stage and actors in a theatre in words that suggest the perspective of someone who has not experienced a theatre before, and who does not know what is going on. The conventions gradually dawn on him, and what dawns on us is the absurd artifice of the theatrical conventions which we had accepted as normal:

The middle of the stage consisted of flat boards; by the sides stood painted pictures representing trees, and at the back a linen cloth was stretched down to the floor boards. Maidens in red bodices and white skirts sat on the middle of the stage. One, very fat, in a white silk dress, sat apart on a narrow bench to which a green pasteboard box was glued from behind. They were all singing something. When they had finished, the maiden in white approached the prompter's box. A man in silk with tightfitting pants on his fat legs approached her with a plume and began to sing and spread his arms in dismay. The man in the tight pants finished his song alone; then the girl sang. After that both remained silent as the music resounded; and the man, obviously waiting to begin singing his part with her again, began to run his fingers over the hand of the girl in the white dress. They finished their song together, and everyone in the theater began to clap and shout. But the men and women on stage, who represented lovers, started to bow, smiling and raising their hands.

Swift uses this technique of uncoding by undercoding repeatedly in *Gulliver's Travels*, with devastating irony. Here is Gulliver's first sight of the Yahoos:

At last I beheld several Animals in a Field, and one or two of the same Kind sitting in Trees. Their Shape was very singular, and deformed, which a little discomposed me, so that I lay down behind a Thicket to observe them better. Some of them coming forward near the Place where I lay, gave me an Opportunity of distinctly marking their Form. Their Heads and Breasts were covered with a thick Hair, some frizzled and others lank; they had Beards like Goats, and a long Ridge of Hair down their Backs, and the fore Parts of their Legs and Feet; but the rest of their Bodies were bare, so that I might see their Skins, which were of a brown Buff Colour. They had no Tails, nor any Hair at all on their Buttocks, except about the Anus; which, I presume Nature has placed there to defend them as they sat on the Ground; for this Posture they used, as well as lying down, and often stood on their hind Feet. They climbed high Trees, as nimbly as a Squirrel, for they had strong extended Claws before and behind, terminating in sharp Points, and hooked. They would often spring, and bound, and leap with prodigious Agility. The Females were not so large as the Males; they had long lank Hair on their Heads, and only a Sort of Down on the rest of their Bodies, except about the Anus, and Pudenda. Their Dugs hung between their fore Feet, and often reached almost to the Ground as they walked. The Hair of both Sexes was of several Colours, brown, red, black and yellow. Upon the whole, I never beheld in all my Travels so disagreeable an Animal, or one against which I naturally conceived so strong an Antipathy.

The Yahoos are of course human beings kept as beasts of burden by the Houyhnhnms. Gulliver first codes them as 'animals', and describes them in meticulous detail as if they were a species of animal never before observed: 'Their Shape was very singular.' What follows is a very straight and literal description in phrases which, we slowly realize, are entirely and accurately applicable to human beings (at least, such human beings as have been exposed to the elements, and do not trim their nails). Gulliver makes clear his disgust, and elicits ours. What he and we are inspecting, with loathing, are in fact human beings, but our perception has been defamiliarized: they are not *labelled* human beings, so we fail to make the usual allowances. This is what people are really like (says Gulliver) if you see them without preconceptions, from an estranged viewpoint unfiltered by the forgiving distortions of 'common sense' and the common terms of ordinary language.

A comic passage from Joyce's *Ulysses* develops this technique of extremely literal and mechanical description but adds a historically distanced style. A modest twentieth-century meal of stout and sardines is depicted with the wide-eyed astonishment of a time-traveller from the fourteenth century:

And in the castle was set a board that was of the birchwood of Finlandy and it was upheld by four dwarfmen of that country but they durst not move for enchantment. And on this board were frightful swords and knives that are made in a great cavern by swinking demons out of white flames that they fix in the horns of buffalos and stags that there abound marvellously. And there were vessels that are wrought by magic of Mahound out of seasand and the air by a warlock with his breath that he blares into them like to bubbles. And full fair cheer and rich was on the board that no wight could devise a fuller ne richer. And there was a vat of silver that was moved by craft to open in the which lay strange fishes withouten heads though misbelieving men nie that this be possible thing without they see it natheless they are so. And these fishes lie in an oily water brought there from Portugal land because of the fatness that therein is like to the juices of the olive press. And also it was marvel to see in that castle how by magic they make a compost out of fecund wheat kidneys out of Chaldee that by aid of certain angry spirits that they do into it swells up wondrously like to a vast mountain. And they teach the serpents there to entwine themselves up on long sticks out of the ground and of the scales of these serpents they brew out a brewage like to mead.

The relevance of these examples to Shklovsky's theory should be clear. In all three, perception of the object of description is delayed: in the first and second cases, by withholding the name of the object, in the third, additionally, by parody of medieval English prose. We experience the described objects as strange, elaborate, artificial rather than familiar, simple, natural. All three—and the second particularly, because of its provocative subject—encourage us to reflect on the artificiality, the constructedness, of our habitual perceptions. The passages make their impact by deliberate linguistic techniques which disturb relationships between signs and meanings; constructing and encoding new meanings.

Startling reorientations of meaning can be achieved in language using very simple devices. In the last stanza of 'The Right of Way' (1923), William Carlos Williams constructs a brilliant *trompe-l'œil*. These are the final three stanzas of the 28-line poem:

> Why bother where I went?
> for I went spinning on the
>
> four wheels of my car
> along the wet road until
>
> I saw a girl with one leg
> over the rail of a balcony

Like the car driver who when he is moving glimpses an object from one position then from another, so that the object changes, the reader first assumes that the penultimate line refers to an amputee, and then as he shifts his attention to the last line is forced to reinterpret completely, restoring the leg. The switch from one interpretation to the other is striking partly because it so neatly mimes a visual process appropriate to the narrative of the poem. Partly also because the connotations of the two interpretations are contradictory: the penultimate line by itself suggests pathos, violence, the grotesque, whereas the complete girl on the balcony implies relaxation and confidence. Also the word 'until' coming after a string of insignificant impressions leads to an expectation of climax: this is what it's all about, the pathos and cruelty of humanity—a climax instantly cancelled when the girl turns out not to be mutilated but just an ordinary person like the figures in the street presented earlier in the poem.

My remarks do not apply to just a first reading. The amputee does not go away even after she has been completed by the final line. The enduring effect is like that of one of those line-drawings of a cube which can be seen either as projecting out from the page towards the viewer or as receding away from him. The drawing switches from one representation to the other unpredictably; either can be seen, but not both together; but while one representation of the cube is being viewed, the possibility of the other can be held in mind. A similar visual ambiguity has been demonstrated with other figures, for example the famous 'duck/rabbit'.

The technique is extensively practised by the fantastic painter Salvador Dali (for example, 'Slave Market with the Apparition of the Invisible Bust of Voltaire', 1940). The effect of such ambiguities is unsettling as well as witty; apprehending one of the two meanings, the reader is always conscious that the cube might switch and impose the second meaning on his attention. The difficulty of perception here is caused by the unstable ambiguity of the sign. This is a very radical kind of defamiliarization which, by insisting that a sign is not tied to *one* meaning, constitutes a critique of the conventionality of signs.

The technique by which William Carlos Williams achieves this particular act of defamiliarization is very simple in its design, quite complicated in its execution. In verse, the sequence of words and phrases can be divided up in two ways. There are the normal syntactic boundaries: between words:

my / car

between phrases:

on the four wheels / of my car

between clauses:

for I went spinning on the four wheels of my car along the wet road / until I saw a girl with one leg over the rail of a balcony

between sentences:

Why bother where I went? / for I went *etc.*

These syntactic divisions have an intuitive psychological reality for speakers of the language, and are felt to divide up the flow of words into units of meaning. There is a second set of segmentations in verse, the line-divisions. These may or may not coincide with major syntactic divisions. Now if the last word in a line *could* be the last word of a syntactic unit, the line-ending encourages the reader to assume that the syntax *does* end there. In our extract, this is impossible with 'the' and 'until', but quite plausible with 'car' and 'leg'. We are bound to try out the hypothesis that 'leg' marks the completion of a unit of meaning; the hypothesis is disconfirmed by what follows but the trace of it never disappears.

Stevens did not invent this device of the ambiguous line-ending: it is conventional—Empson in *Seven Types of Ambiguity* has examples from Shakespeare. The question arises how the convention works so powerfully and freshly here, how it avoids the staleness of an old conjuring trick. (All creative practice has this precarious relationship with convention: the twin dangers are diminishing returns and obviousness of technique, both products of the over-use of some conventional technique. The dangers are particularly acute for 'modernist' practitioners like Williams, Dali, Brecht, Apollinaire, Satie, Weill, who systematically exploit and draw attention to conventions of illusion.) To answer the question properly would demand a detailed analysis of the whole poem, which is not possible here, but I can indicate some of the elements briefly.

One part of the answer is that the semantic unit 'I saw a girl with one leg' is *motivated*—it is a reasonable climax in terms of the poem's thematic and narrative structure. The speaker in the poem has been driving along catching sight of some mundane, morally unremarkable scenes; he and we are due for a shock. But the main cause of the success of this device is more strictly linguistic. For various metrical reasons (including the shortness of the lines, the presence of one-syllable words at the ends of many lines, the typographical format which frames the text with areas of blank page), the line-boundaries are either very salient or potentially so. This means that they can readily be used to 'punctuate' the sentence-structure—as happens in the penultimate line. Though the metre tends towards interruption at regular brief intervals, the syntax favours long, cumulative sentences. The syntax is what linguists call *'right-branching'*: phrases and clauses are added to the right of the main clause one after the other, each dependent on the one immediately before:

> for I went spinning
>     on the four wheels
>         of my car
>             along the wet road
> until I saw a girl
>     with one leg
>         over the rail
>             of a balcony

The syntax carries the reader's attention forward in a large sweep broader than the short lines. Although the constituent phrases are roughly the same length as the material lines, very few of them coincide with the lines, as comparison of the above informal diagram with the text of the poem will show. Not only does Williams avoid matching line-ends and phrase-ends; he also produces a sort of 'negative correlation' by ending some lines with words that demand syntactic continuation, emphasizing forward movement in the reader's attention: 'on the/', 'until/'. There is a background of enjambment (run-on lines) against which any potential coincidence of line-break and syntactic boundary is strongly foregrounded. A related structural feature is the scarcity of lines which are syntactically and semantically complete; exceptionally, 'I saw a girl with one leg' is a complete clause, and its completeness, reinforced by the line-break, claims the reader's notice.

So Williams puts together basically dissimilar and divergent metrical and syntactic patterns, resists coincidence of boundaries so that when they ultimately do appear to converge the sense of delayed completion is particularly strong. Then, such is the fluidity of the language of this poem that the climax is immediately undone by the final two phrases which change the reader's over-confident syntactic analysis of the penultimate line. But this analysis—'a girl with one leg'—can never be finally erased: it is validated partly by the potential end-stopping, and also by a property of the right-branching syntax which dominates the poem. In right-branching syntax, modifying phrases are added as 'extras' on the end (the right), and can be removed without damaging the wholeness of what precedes (you can test this by going back to the diagram and stripping away phrases starting from the bottom right). It is as if the added phrases are not really necessary . . . so perhaps 'I saw a girl with one leg' is 'really' complete after all. We can never be sure. The poem is distinguished by the openness of interpretation, the witty anti-dogmatism, which its formal structure encourages.

I want now to return briefly to the couplet by Pope to which only a provisional and informal response was given at the beginning of Chapter 2:

> Not louder Shrieks to pitying Heav'n are cast,
> When Husbands or when Lap-dogs breathe their last.

A social judgement is passed here, an indictment of fashionable women who value their lapdogs as much as they do their husbands, and, by implication, devalue their husbands by giving the same degree of affection to people, who ought to be greatly loved, and pets, which merit little attachment. Readers familiar with *The Rape of the Lock* will know that this judgement is only part of a general attack on the levelling of values—sexual, religious, material, political—the degrading of people, relationships, and standards by taking them down to the lowest level, equating them with trivial material possessions—dogs, jewellery, ornaments. Compare:

> Whether the Nymph shall break Diana's Law,
> Or some frail China Jar receive a Flaw,
> Or stain her Honour, or her new Brocade,
> Forget her Pray'rs, or miss a Masquerade,
> Or lose her Heart, or Necklace, at a Ball;
> Or whether Heav'n has doom'd that Shock must fall.

Or:

> Here Thou, Great Anna! whom three Realms obey,
> Dost sometimes Counsel take—and sometimes Tea.

We are not concerned here with the satirical theme of the poem. The point is that a consistent set of propositions are being implied here, which are not the statements affirmed by the normal linear syntax of the poem: indeed, the implications made between the lines are at odds with the assertions made by the actual sentences. As in 'The Right of Way', the effect is achieved by extra, metrical, operations on language superimposed upon the underlying prose syntax. (Of course, the effects are quite different in the two poems, and the metrical devices are absolutely different, but the overall technical principle is the same.) In the case of Pope, the recoding is done by means of his dominant technique of creating equivalent metrical positions. Rhyming words, or in these examples parallel nouns in equivalent places in the first and second halves of lines, take on *semantic* relationships. The words 'Husbands' and 'Lap-dogs' are both two-syllable words with the same stress pattern; both appear after the lightly stressed 'when'. Their phonetic equivalence (similarity of sound and metrical placing) suggests semantic equivalence (the social concept 'husband' has the same value as the social concept 'lapdog'). Similarly, 'prayers' = 'masquerade', 'counsel' = 'tea', etc.

Now I want to make a further observation which would not emerge if we took the husbands/lapdogs example just by itself. Pope does not create his insight into degrading matrons of the 1700s autonomously within this particular couplet. The technique of language which is used to express this insight—the sensitization of certain metrical positions so that they establish new equivalences and contrasts of meaning—is a stylistic code which is built up in the poem as a whole, Pope's verse as a whole, Pope's predecessors in the heroic couplet verse form. This stylistic code is an extra over and above the regular code of the language. Now a reader cannot get the illumination expressed by the husbands/lapdogs line unless he knows this code. In the same way, readers need to have learned something of the conventional significances of enjambment and end-stopping in order to appreciate the full force of the visual ambiguity in the Williams poem.

We can see that there is a paradoxical process working here. Defamiliarization, or creation of meaning, is achieved by using a stylistic code to criticize the limitations of the existing linguistic code. But, because the technique of metrical balance which performs the critique is itself a code, a set of repeatable conventions, it is subject to the law of diminishing returns and must decay into a meaningless habit. And this is exactly what happened to the various conventional techniques of Augustan verse as the eighteenth century progressed. Through repeated use they became meaningless. For instance, one technique was the frequent use of adjectives to qualify the meanings of nouns, so that it became unusual to use a noun without specifying its meaning further. In principle, this is an excellent critical practice, leading to precision and resisting acceptance of the noun as an unanalysed category. In practice, repetition led to cliché and vacuousness. A poem like 'Ode' by Mark Akenside (1721–70) will illustrate the depths to which the technique sank. The first two stanzas go:

> On yonder verdant hillock laid,
> Where oaks and elms, a friendly shade,
>  O'erlook the falling stream,
> O master of the Latin lyre,
> Awhile with thee I will retire,
>  From summer's noontide beam.
>
> And, lo, within my lonely bower,
> The industrious bee from many a flower

Collects her balmy dews:
'For me', she sings, 'the gems are born,
For me their silken robe adorn,
Their fragrant breath diffuse.'

The adjective + noun phrases in the remaining six stanzas are as follows:

sweet murmurer, rude storm, hospitable scene, gladsome toils, ambrosial spoils, lowly, silvan scenes, flowery greens, fond ambition, boding raven, unhallowed haunts, horrid glooms, barren waste, lurking strength, noxious thing, insipid nightshade, baneful juice, sordid sting, vernal blooms, blameless wealth, generous task, double boon.

'Ambrosial spoils' (nectar) is a dead metaphorical cliché like the notorious 'finny tribes' (fish), symbol of what went wrong with eighteenth-century poetic diction. Most of these phrases are not of that kind, though. They are, simply, redundant and vacuous: the adjective contributes no meaning, for all bees are industrious, all blooms are vernal, all storms rude, and so on. The phrase 'barren waste' (i.e. desert, waste land) is typical: since all wastes are by definition barren, it adds nothing to say that they are barren. The phrase is a tautology, and one feels that the adjective slot has been filled not for semantic precision but out of a mere syntactic habit. What began, in earlier years, as a device for saying something fresh has become a mechanical pattern with no conceptual force.

One task of linguistic criticism would be to study the atrophy of linguistic techniques from creative illumination to automatic and meaningless pattern. The aim of such criticism would not be destructive—though it would be unlikely to convert modern readers to Akenside. There are a number of interesting historical studies to be done on these passages of language into unthinking habit. However, a more important role for criticism is to keep alive what is permanently worthwhile in the creative phases of particular linguistic codes. There is a danger that Pope's techniques can lose their force not through any inherent defects but because our response has been contaminated by our knowledge of the later, mechanical, phase of eighteenth-century syntax and versification. It can happen that we are no longer able to see how Pope's poetic technique creatively criticizes the assumptions encoded in the language of his time; and linguistic criticism comes into the picture with the role of resuscitating the original techniques for the jaded and perhaps cynical modern reader.

## Notes

1. 'Art as Technique', in Lee T. Lemon and Marion J. Reis, trans., *Russian Formalist Criticism: Four Essays* (Lincoln: University of Nebraska Press, 1965), pp. 11, 12.
2. 'Thematics', in Lemon and Reis, p. 85.

# 5

# How Texts are Made

This chapter, as its title suggests, is about some really basic aspects of linguistic structure: parts of language, and arrangements of language, which are in use in all our experience of language, written or spoken, in any situation from jokey conversation to high epic. The fact that they are ordinary, constant, background features of language does not mean that they are unimportant in literature. Without the basic devices for constructing texts, none of the specialized techniques which are found in much modern literature would be possible.

Let's start with two fundamental units: *sentence* and *text*. I shall be discussing both types of units, since texts consist of sentences linked together in ways that are described in this and the following chapter. Details of sentence structure will be mentioned throughout the book, but for a full treatment readers are referred to the introductory books on linguistics recommended on p. 183. On the whole, other linguists have concentrated on individual sentences, but we are concerned with how sentences work in longer stretches of text. As a concrete example, I can illustrate some of the processes by reference to the opening paragraphs of the novel *Cat's Cradle* (1963) by Kurt Vonnegut, Jr.:

1. Call me Jonah. 2. My parents did, or nearly did. 3. They called me John.
    4. Jonah—John—if I had been a Sam, I would have been a Jonah still —not because I have been unlucky for others, but because somebody or something has compelled me to be certain places at certain times, without fail. 5. Conveyances and motives, both conventional and bizarre, have been provided. 6. And, according to plan, at each appointed second, at each appointed place this Jonah was there.
    7. Listen:
    8. When I was a younger man—two wives ago, 250,000 cigarettes ago, 3,000 quarts of booze ago . . .
    9. When I was a much younger man, I began to collect material for a book to be called *The Day the World Ended*.
    10. The book was to be factual.

11. The book was to be an account of what important Americans had done on the day when the first atomic bomb was dropped on Hiroshima, Japan.
12. It was to be a Christian book. 13. I was a Christian then.
14. I am a Bokononist now.

The traditional thing to say about a *sentence* is that it 'expresses a complete thought'. This is correct, but vague. This 'thought', from the point of view of linguistics or of logic, is a *proposition*. A proposition is a combination of a word or words which *refer* to, or could refer to, entities in the world ('Jonah', 'my parents', 'conveyances', 'a book') with a word or words which *predicates* an action, a state or a process of the entities referred to ('call', 'unlucky', 'compelled'). The referring words are usually nouns, the predicating words usually verbs or adjectives, though, as we shall see, these are tendencies only, and found in only the simplest sentences. In sentence 10, the proposition neatly fits the structure of a simple sentence:

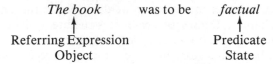

Similarly, sentence 3 joins three referring expressions and a predicate together in one proposition which is expressed in a simple sentence:

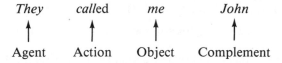

The terms 'agent', 'object', 'complement', 'state', 'action' belong to a small and highly important basic semantic vocabulary for analysing the roles of the participants referred to by nouns, and the types of activities and situations described by the verbs that go with them. The importance of this part of the analysis of sentence meanings lies in the fact that agency, state, process, and so on seem to be the basic categories in terms of which human beings present the world to themselves through language. We think of the world, and speak and write about it, as a collection of objects: some animate, some inanimate, acting, moving, changing, causing change in other things, or just being or continuing in a certain state or condition. Literary writings may confirm such assumptions, or challenge them. We will analyse some aspects of this area of meaning in Chapters 9 and 10.

To return to the 'fit' of propositions and sentences, this is very often less straightforward than it is in the simple sentences 3 and 10 (or 12–14). Sentence 1 illustrates a characteristic complication in the process of expressing propositions: less than the whole proposition is stated; one of the referring expressions has been deleted and part of the verb phrase, but our knowledge of English syntax tells us what they must be: '/You will/ call me Jonah.' Here three referring expressions, 'you', 'me' and 'Jonah', are linked with the predicate, 'call'. The proposition itself is complete; by a syntactic convention of English, it is not entirely expressed.

Many sentences express more than one proposition. Sometimes the component propositions are clearly visible as separate clauses, as for example 'I was a much younger man' and 'I began to collect material' in sentence 9. Often, however, their parts are shuffled around and deleted to the extent that the underlying propositional parts of a sentence are barely observable on the surface. (I am not saying that this causes any particular difficulty for readers; this is simply a syntactic fact about sentences, and readers know the syntax and so can 'decode' transformations of propositions which look rather complicated when they are pointed out.) Sentence 5 of our passage, for instance, is formed from a series of propositions which are not distinctly visible as separate clauses in the surface shape of the sentence; roughly:

Somebody has provided conveyances for me.
Somebody has provided motives for me.
Some of the conveyances were conventional.
Some of the conveyances were bizarre.
Some of the motives were conventional.
Some of the motives were bizarre.

Listing the propositions like this, as separate sentences, is meant to display all the semantic components that are dovetailed together in the real sentence, showing all the parts rather in the manner that an 'exploded' mechanical drawing of, say, a car gearbox does. We can see the degree of compression involved in constructing a complex sentence out of several propositions. Ideas that occur twice in the semantic structure ('provided', etc.) are not mentioned twice in the completed sentence; and ideas which are implicit are not mentioned at all—for example, the participants 'somebody' and 'me' which are essential to the meaning but quite suppressed in sentence 5, though they are specified in the previous sentence.

Something else which emerges when one divides a sentence into its propositional constituents is that these *might* have been fitted together in some different arrangement:

Somebody has provided both conventional and bizarre conveyances and motives.

This rewriting makes much the same sense as the original sentence. Why then does Vonnegut put it his way rather than some other way? For instance, why does he use the passive 'conveyances . . . have been provided' rather than the active which would have been consistent with the previous sentence—'somebody . . . has compelled me to be certain places . . . Somebody has provided . . . conveyances . . .'? Such questions cannot be answered without extensive and close study of the text, of course. The point to be noted here is that the transformational reordering and assembling of separate propositions into complex sentences provide alternative wordings which may have different effects. The kind of analysis which is offered by transformational grammar is extremely useful in discussing these effects.

To recapitulate. A sentence consists of one or more propositions. The semantic function of propositions is referring and predicating: referring to entities (real or imaginary) and predicating actions, states or processes of them. Obviously, a proposition is an abstract unit of meaning and so there is a process of 'realization' or 'expression' between the abstract idea and the concrete sentential form. Propositions must be expressed syntactically as the regularly ordered sequences of words and phrases which comprise sentences. The processes of combination, rearrangement, deletion, and so on which intervene between propositional meaning and syntactic form are known as *transformations*. There can be transformationally different arrangements of the same set of propositions, leading to different effects of the meaning, or different perspectives on the meaning.

Before turning to the larger unit of structure, *text*, I want to mention three further aspects of sentence-meaning and sentence-form: *Speech acts, modality*, and *deixis*.

First, sentences are used not only to convey propositions but also to perform *speech acts*.[1] In our text, for example, sentences 1 and 7 differ from all the rest in being commands, the others being assertions or representatives through which the narrator begins to relate the story which Vonnegut has constructed out of a series of fictional propositions. The range of speech acts in our extract is limited—there are no questions, for example—but we will look at a greater range in Chapter 8.

Another property of sentences, somewhat related to speech acts, is *modality*: the degree of assurance or commitment with which a speaker vouches for a proposition. From the confidence (but irony) of the famous opening sentence of Jane Austen's *Pride and Prejudice* (1813):

It is a truth universally acknowledged, that a single man in possession of a good fortune, must be in want of a wife.

to the wavering uncertainty of the narrator's reflections on the origin of his fear of closed doors at the beginning of Joseph Heller's *Something Happened!* (1974):

Maybe it was the day I came home unexpectedly with a fever and a sore throat and caught my father in bed with my mother that left me with my fear of doors, my fear of opening doors and my suspicion of closed ones. Or maybe it was the knowledge that . . . Or the day my father died . . . Or maybe it was the realization . . . Or maybe it was the day I did open another door and saw my big sister standing naked . . .

The modalities which an author gives to his narrators, or to the speaker in a poem, characterize their authority or 'presence', and, in narrative, the point of view they adopt towards the subject matter, whether omniscient, confident, or partial, tentative. See further, Chapter 9.

Finally, to propositions, transformations, speech acts, and modality as properties of sentences we must add *deixis*. This—the Greek word for 'pointing'—refers to the orientation of the content of a sentence in relation to time, place, and personal participants. Suppose you and I are together in a specific place, and I say to you: 'We're going there right now', referring to some other

place that we both know about. The deictic parts of the sentence
locate the proposition within the real world in which we communicate: 'we' establishes that it is the speaker and the addressee
who are the subject of the discourse; 'there' links our destina-
tion to the place of utterance, '-'re going' announces future time
in relation to the time of utterance, and 'right now' further
qualifies it as immediate future time. By these deictic devices the
message is made directly relevant to the personal and the spatio-
temporal situation of the utterance. In written language there is
deixis also, but its force is different from that of the orienting
devices of speech, because the source and the addressee do not
normally occupy the same place in space and time—except in
cases such as a note passed in a meeting. With literary texts
there are additional complications: the author does not know
who the reader is, the reader usually does not know the author,
the author may be several hundred years dead, the 'speaker' or
narrator in a literary text is anyway not a real person and not the
actual writer. In *Cat's Cradle*, the narrator pretends that there is
a common point of time, a 'present', which he and the reader
share, and that there is a future for both (sentences 1, 7, and 14)
—this is in retrospect reassuring or ironic, since at the end of
the novel we know that the narrator has survived the end of the
world! Between sentences 1 and 14 several time-levels are indicated: a time before that of the narration, the time of the narrator's parents (2–3); a general past time covering the whole of
the narrator's life 'so far' (4–6); and a specific past sometime
after 1945; the beginning of the relevant narrated time (8–13)
including a prospective future between 'then' and 'now' ('to be',
'was to be', 9–12). There is thus a complicated, and plausible,
time-scheme evoked by the deictic elements of this sequence of
sentences—and a narratively *interesting* scheme, because the
juxtaposition of 13 and 14 implies that something happened
which changed, probably aborted, the hypothetical future indicated by 9–12.

   *Place* is not deictically relevant in this extract. There are no
indicators of the location of the speaker or addressee. *Person* is
important, however. The imperatives of 1 and 7 strongly (if
counter-factually) evoke an individual speaker, an individual
addressee, and an intimate relationship between them; this fictive
personal link is the beginning of the making of a colloquial and

jokey style appropriate to the comic apocalypse of which the novel tells.

The above are some of the main headings under which we describe the structure of sentences, and they are also features of structure which are potentially significant when discussing larger units, texts—this will become obvious in the later, descriptive, chapters. But a theoretical point was made at the beginning of this chapter to the effect that a text is a different kind of unit from a sentence. A *text* is made up of sentences, but there exist separate principles of text-construction, beyond the rules for making sentences. We now turn to these principles.

Let's begin with an example. It might as well be from this very text: say, this sentence and the three preceding ones. If we extract any single sentence—for example, 'We now turn to these principles'—it is linguistically interpretable as a proposition out of its context, but it only makes practical sense within its context. The deictic word 'these' points back to the preceding sentence, identifying which principles are being referred to. Similarly, 'an example' harks back to 'these principles': an example *of what*? Every example must be an example of something—an example 'of these principles'. Then 'It' in 'It might as well . . .' refers to 'an example', and, after the colon, 'this sentence' replaces 'It' and connects with 'an example'. There are other types of connection in this stretch of text. The word 'principles' is repeated, referring to the *same* principles. Syntactically, 'We' is implicitly reiterated in 'Let's', and then repeated (with the same reference: the author and his assumed reader) in the following sentence. The verb 'turn', in this context, must mean something like 'move to consider a new section of the argument'; this meaning is developed in the next verb, 'begin'. Note that, considered in isolation, the two words have little in common, but in this textual context the second picks up and builds on the meaning of the first.

We may return (note the cohesive ties with the above) to *Cat's Cradle* for a second example, for more instances of structure above the sentence. Sentence 1 is the first sentence of the novel and does not connect with any immediately preceding co-text.[2] Sentence 2 could not exist without sentence 1: 2 presupposes (as part of its meaning: 'My parents [called me Jonah], or nearly [called me Jonah].' It seems that omission, or ellipsis, is a text-structure device; that what is stated in one sentence may be left unsaid in the next, the silence being a signal of the coherence of the text, its focus on a single topic. Note that 'did' is what might be called a *pro-verb*, standing for the verb phrase 'call me Jonah' rather as a *pronoun* stands for a noun phrase—cf. 'They' = 'My parents' linking 3 with 2, or 'It' = 'The book' linking 12 and 11. Other straightforward linking devices include lexical repetition: 'Jonah . . . Jonah', 'The book . . . The book', 'places . . . place'; and lexical variation: 'times . . . second'. But there are also some very much more complicated textual relationships in evidence here. How is it that we know that sentences 4–6 develop the same idea, that of the narrator as victim of forces which move him beyond his control?

4. . . . because somebody or something has compelled me to be certain places at certain times, without fail. 5. Conveyances and motives, both conventional and bizarre, have been provided. 6. And, according to plan, at each appointed second, at each appointed place this Jonah was there.

Our assumption of logical and narrative continuity derives partly from transformational syntax. We assume that the deleted agent and patient of 'provided' and 'appointed' are the same as those explicitly given for 'compelled'; the nominalization (verb-turned-noun) 'plan' has the same implied syntax: 'somebody planned for me.' By association, the idea of compulsion against the will extends from 'compelled' to 'provided', 'plan', and 'appointed'. There are other ties among this sequence of sentences. 'Conveyances', for instance, develops the idea of movement to 'certain places' in the preceding sentence, and looks forward to the repeated 'place' in the following one. We could find further links, but by now the general point is surely clear. Not only do sentences have their own individual meanings and their rules for the possible structures for expressing these meanings, they are also, in texts, linked to one another by a complex network of ties involving numerous different parts of language structure—vocabulary, pronouns, syntactic deletions, etc.

When we read a newspaper article or a novel, or listen to someone talking or reading a poem aloud, we bring certain expectations about what counts as 'sensible communication'. Texts are organized in relation to these expectations. We expect texts to be coherent, to stay on one topic and not jump unexpectedly from subject to subject; to take another term from Hallidayan linguistics, we expect *cohesion*.[3] Second, we expect texts not to repeat the same point constantly but to present a developing argument or narrative. That is, we expect the propositions in a cohesive text to be arranged to make a *progressive* sequence of ideas. So strong is this assumption of progression that we normally interpret a pair of sentences as logically or chronologically related even if such a relationship is not overtly stated. For instance, if someone says 'John had 'flu. He couldn't attend the meeting,' we automatically assume that John's 'flu started *before* the meeting and that he didn't attend the meeting *because* of his 'flu. Finally, in addition to cohesion and progression, we expect *thematization*. This is organization of the text so as to draw attention to the most important parts of its content, its themes. There are numerous devices for doing this, including attention-catching transformations of word-order: 'I like peas and beans, but *carrots* I can't stand.' Illustrations are difficult without quoting lengthy texts, but any unexpected ruffling of the surface of the text by noticeable phonology, printing, syntax, or vocabulary is potentially thematizing. There are many literary conventions for thematization, some illustrated in other chapters of this book.

Of these three basic aspects of textual structure, I shall concentrate on the one which seems to be fundamental to the organization of texts, *cohesion*. Cohesion distinguishes well-formed texts, focusing on an integrated topic, with well-signalled internal transitions, from arbitrary and inconsequential strings of sentences. It is founded on a very simple principle: each sentence after the first is linked to the content of one or more preceding sentences by at least one *tie*. A tie is made by some constituent which resumes, reiterates or otherwise recalls something designated by a predicate or a referring expression in a preceding sentence. Thus:

Call me Jonah. My parents did. Or nearly did. They called me John.

Call me Jonah. My parents did. Or nearly did. They called me John.

Call me Jonah. My parents did. Or nearly did. They called me John.

Call me Jonah. My parents did. Or nearly did. They called me John.

Call me Jonah. My parents did. Or nearly did. They called me John.

Call me Jonah. My parents did. Or nearly did. They called me John.

Call me Jonah. My parents did. Or [my parents] nearly did. They called me John.

Call me Jonah. My parents did. Or nearly did. They called me John.

The diagram shows how many cohesive ties exist even in a very short and simple text. Every part of the third sentence is prepared for by some element of a preceding one. It also demonstrates that ties are of a number of kinds; for example, the link between *did* and *Call me Jonah* is quite different from that between *my* and *me*.

Halliday and Hasan distinguish five kinds of cohesive relationship linking sentences:

### (i) *Reference*

A word in a subsequent sentence, usually a pronoun (*he, she, it*) or a demonstrative (*this, that*), refers to some entity or action that has been designated by another term in a preceding sentence (my italics in the following examples):

Stately, plump *Buck Mulligan* came from the stairhead, bearing a bowl of lather on which a mirror and a razor lay crossed. A yellow dressinggown, ungirdled, was sustained gently behind *him* by the mild morning air. *He* held the bowl aloft and intoned:

(James Joyce, *Ulysses*, 1922)

As to these points, *Jenny satisfied him by the most solemn assurances*, that the man was entirely out of his reach, and was neither subject to his power, nor in any probability of becoming an object of his goodness.
   The ingenuity of *this behaviour*, had gained Jenny so much credit with this worthy man, that he easily believed what she told him . . .

(Henry Fielding, *Tom Jones*, 1749)

### (ii) *Substitution*

Here a word in the second sentence refers not to exactly the same entity as does the related word in the first, but to some other entity to which the same term would be applicable. Halliday and Hasan's example:

Would you like this *teapot*?
—No, I want a square *one*.

Here the continuity is based not on two references to the same teapot, but two mentions of the concept 'teapot' referring to two different instances. Substitution works with verbs as well as nouns, the commonest verbal substitutes being 'do' ('did') and 'do so' ('did so'). In our Vonnegut example, sentence 2, the pro-verb (cf. 'pronoun') 'did' substitutes for the whole of the verb phrase 'call me Jonah'. As with the teapot example, the same thing, or event, is not being referred to twice. First it is the reader being exhorted to call the narrator Jonah, then his parents nearly called him Jonah.

## (iii) *Ellipsis*

This is one use of what would be called 'deletion' in transformational terms. A part of a subsequent sentence which would repeat a phrase or idea explicitly stated in a preceding sentence is omitted, making the second sentence depend for its completeness on the first; in the following, I have reinserted the deleted repetitions in square brackets:

He descended upon North Beach like a chapter from the Old Testament. He was the reason birds migrate in the autumn. They have to [migrate in the autumn]. He was the cold turning of the earth; [he was] the bad wind that blows off sugar.

(Richard Brautigan, *The Shipping of Trout Fishing in America Shorty to Nelson Algren*, 1967)

Ellipsis is a very important cohesive device in dialogue, a guarantee that speakers are concentrating together on a single topic and on the background knowledge relevant to the topic. In fictional dialogue, ellipsis suggests intimacy, intensity. (In the following examples I have placed empty square brackets at the points of deletion and not supplied the deleted words, to avoid distorting the text too much.)

'I know what *you* want,' she said.
*I* know what I want,' he said. 'What's the odds?'
'Well, you're not going to have it off *me*.'
'Aren't I [ ]? Well, then I'm not [ ]. It's no use crying about it, is it?'
'No, it isn't [ ],' said the girl, rather disconcerted by his irony. . . .
'Where have you been?' she asked, puzzled, interested.
'[ ] to the Empire.'

'Who [ ] with?'
'[ ] By myself. I came home with Tom Cooper.'

(D. H. Lawrence, *The Rainbow*, 1915)

### (iv) *Lexical cohesion*

The cohesive techniques we have looked at so far have drawn on syntactic processes—substitution of pronouns, pro-verbs, transformational deletion, etc. Additionally, fully meaningful vocabulary items—referring and predicating expressions, nouns and verbs—contribute to textual cohesion, in two ways:

(a) *Lexical reiteration.*   This is like reference and substitution, only using full words rather than pronouns or other substitutes. The same word is repeated in a subsequent sentence, either referring to the same object (cf. 'reference') or to another instance of an object of the same kind (cf. 'substitution'). In the passage from *Ulysses*:

Stately, plump Buck Mulligan came from the stairhead, bearing a *bowl* . . . He held the *bowl* aloft . . .

and

from the *stairhead* . . . he peered down the dark winding *stairs* . . .

where 'stairs' varies the 'stairhead' reference as well as repeating it. Variation may be taken a stage further, with the second word being a close synonym of the first. Halliday gives an example from Leslie Stephen:

Accordingly, after a peace-offering of tobacco, in return for a draught of foaming milk, I took leave, and turned to the *ascent* of the peak.
    The *climb* is perfectly easy, though I contrived to complicate matters by going the wrong way.

(b) *Collocation.*   Sets of words tend to turn up together in texts because they relate to the same idea: 'ice', 'snow', 'freeze', 'white', 'frost', 'blizzard'; 'electricity', 'amp', 'circuit', 'charge', 'switch'. They *collocate*: members of the same lexical set tend to appear close together in texts because texts tend to be cohesive, to stay on the same topic. 'Frost' goes with 'snow' not only in the vocabulary structure of the language considered abstractly, but in real texts expressing real meanings:

*Outlook*: Wintry showers in many places at first, becoming mainly dry in the South. Sunny intervals, cold, with night frost, becoming less cold later (*Guardian*, 29 January 1979).

Collocation is a natural and unnoticed aspect of textual cohesiveness (but no less important for that). In a weather forecast, a very high density of meteorological terms is expected and makes no impact; similarly, a chemist will find nothing abnormal in a scientific article being full of chemical terms, though (and this may be a clue to what happens in literature) a layman may well find that usage extremely defamiliarizing. For the chemist, the high density is usual given the context he supplies for the text; the layman cannot supply exactly the right context and therefore the text is odd. The defamiliarizing effects of lexical collocation in literary texts result from the fact that the context is *not* given in advance and so the reader has to construct a context which makes sense of the lexical patterns.

One example of the significance of lexical collocation will serve at this point (the technique is also illustrated in Chapter 6 below). Let us extend the *Ulysses* passage a little:

*Stately*, plump Buck Mulligan came from the stairhead, bearing a bowl of lather on which a mirror and a razor lay **crossed**. A yellow dressing-gown, **ungirdled**, was sustained gently behind him by the mild morning air. He held the bowl aloft and **intoned**:
—**Introibo ad altare Dei.**
Halted, he peered down the dark winding stairs and called up coarsely:
—Come up, Kinch.   Come up, you fearful **jesuit**.
*Solemnly* he came forward and *mounted* the round gunrest. He faced about and **blessed gravely** thrice the tower, the surrounding country and the awaking mountains. Then, catching sight of Stephen Dedalus, he bent towards him and made rapid **crosses** in the air, gurgling in his throat and shaking his head. Stephen Dedalus, displeased and sleepy, leaned his arms on the top of the staircase and looked coldly at the shaking gurgling face that **blessed** him, equine in its length, and at the light **untonsured** hair, grained and hued like pale oak.

The words in bold type are collocates from the terminology of the Roman Catholic church; those in italics are compatible terms suggesting the gravity of a religious ceremony. Buck Mulligan does a parodic imitation of the Mass within the profane context of two very secular young men getting up, shaving, cooking their breakfast in the martello tower in which they lodge. The mock ceremony is intimated by the lexical collocations as well as narrated by the propositions of the sentences. The half-comic, half-disturbing tone of the scene is a result of defamiliarizing shifts and breaches of lexical cohesion: the intrusion within the religious vocabulary of a clashing lexis of brisk and physical motion—'rapid', 'gurgling', 'shaking', 'shaking', 'gurgling'—and the unexpected metaphor 'equine' which is both grotesque and implicitly blasphemous. Note also the oddity of a *face*, rather than a whole person or the mind or spirit of a person, performing a blessing. Naturally, lexical collocation, its developments and deviations, has a strong influence on the structuring of ideas in a text.

### (v) *Conjunction*

Sequences of sentence cohere—and *progress*, cf. p. 61 above—by various semantic relationships between them. As the following example, illustrating *temporal succession*, shows, these relationships hold between the clauses within a sentence as well as the sentences within a text:

I wrote the address down on a piece of paper and pushed the directory back across the desk. The negro put it back where he had found it, shook hands with me, then folded his hands on the desk exactly where they had been when I came in. His eyes drooped slowly and he appeared to fall asleep.

(Raymond Chandler, *Farewell, My Lovely*, 1940)

Besides temporal succession, there are various logical conjunctive relationships which Halliday and Hasan classify into three types:

(a) *Additive.* A succeeding sentence supplies some additional information about a topic:

The book was to be factual . . . It was to be a Christian book. He descended upon North Beach . . . He was the reason . . .

(b) *Adversative.* The second sentence is in an oppositional or contrastive relationship with the first, expressing one of the adversative semantic relationships such as 'yet', 'nevertheless', 'but', 'despite', etc.:

He was totally blind. Yet they had been very happy.

(D. H. Lawrence, 'The Blind Man')

Shall I compare thee to a summer's day?
Thou art more lovely and more temperate:
(Shakespeare, Sonnet 18)

The logical relationship between the first two lines of this sonnet is contrastive: there is an implicit 'no' between them, unstated— note that these conjunctive relationships do not need to be expressed in an actual conjunctive word.[4]

(c) *Causal.* Here the relationships are 'if . . . then', 'because', 'therefore', etc.; once again they may or may not be stated explicitly in a conjunction. Expressed:

Fanny asked her mother numerous small questions, all having nothing to do with 'the subject, which a wise person would have perceived was occupying her attention. Consequently, she received many short answers.

(Elizabeth Gaskell, *North and South*, 1854-5)

Unexpressed causation:

I drove fast. I needed a drink badly and the bars were closed . . .

I was hungry. I went down to the Mansion House Coffee Shop and ate lunch . . .

(*Farewell, My Lovely*)

Interestingly, I found it very hard to find clear examples of expressed causal conjunction in *Farewell, My Lovely*. There are a great many implicit causatives in Chandler, like the above examples, and these may contribute to the overall terseness of his style, the impression that the reader has constantly to retrieve unstated assumptions to understand Marlowe's reasoning and motives. There are also numerous equivocal or even paradoxical explicit causatives:

1. I walked along to the double doors and stood in front of them. 2. They were motionless now. 3. It wasn't any of my business. 4. So I pushed them open and looked in.

The conclusion in 4 is warranted by the observation in 2, but is inconsistent with the immediately preceding proposition in 3: more appropriate would be the adversative conjunction 'nevertheless'. Such contradictions as this, ironized by Marlowe, help shape Chandler's characterization of his hero–narrator as reckless, hasty, uncalculating, and humorously fatalistic. Once again, we find an arrangement at the level of textual structure contributing to the experiential meaning of a text.

## Notes

1. See J. R. Searle, *Speech Acts* (London: Cambridge University Press, 1969); M. L. Pratt, *Toward a Speech Act Theory of Literary Discourse* (Bloomington: Indiana University Press, 1977).
2. It alludes to the biblical story of Jonah and the whale (cf. sentence 4) and to the first sentence of Ch. 1 of *Moby Dick*, 'Call me Ishmael', but these allusions, though important and complicated in their effect, are not part of textual structure; they belong to *pragmatics*.
3. M. A. K. Halliday and Ruqaiya Hasan, *Cohesion in English* (London: Longman, 1976).
4. Conjunctive relationships of all kinds are enormously important in the rhetorical structure of Shakespeare's Sonnets—linking individual lines, quatrain to quatrain, and the final couplet to the sum of the three preceding quatrains. They are also very prominent in heroic couplet verse such as Pope's. These are simple but very rich materials through which the reader could study the poetic significance of just one feature of textual structure.

# 6
## Extra Structure, Extra Meanings

In the previous chapter I introduced some basic features of textual organization which reflect conditions for any 'sensible communication' through language. Whether it be an informal conversation or a formal paper, a text is a sequence of sentences. A sentence is a syntactic unit but the syntax, the ordering of words and phrases, is semantically based; its function is to make meanings tangible as signs arranged in space (writing) or time (speech). The core of meaning is the proposition, which refers to entities in the world as categorized by the language community, and which predicates properties of these entities. Sentences are used to perform speech acts such as stating, questioning, and commanding, and, in more specialized contexts, promising, marrying, betting, etc. The speaker also communicates his attitudes towards the probability, desirability, and so on, of the states of affairs mentioned in the propositions (modality). Additionally, the utterance of a sentence contains indicators of the spatial, temporal, and interpersonal orientation of its content (deixis).

We saw also that, in continuous text, sentences are linked together by an intricate system of cohesive ties. Textual cohesion distinguishes a well-formed text from a random list of sentences. A cohesive text stays on its topic or makes clear shifts of topic, develops a subject rationally and indicates what are the prominent and the subordinate parts of an argument or a story. The complexity of cohesion and related text-structural devices is only just beginning to be recognized by linguists; their importance, once acknowledged, is evidently very great. The reader can test this importance by taking any text quoted in the previous chapter and jumbling its sentences into another order, noticing the incoherence that is produced and considering what cohesive ties have been destroyed by the rearrangement. Radical dislocation of cohesion is of course a conventional strategy in some kinds of writing, for example the *nouveau roman*; I am not hostile to this degree of uncohesiveness, but merely wish to point out just how fundamental the cohesive apparatus is, and so how radical any disruption of it is.

The next stage of my argument does not depend on a notion of 'disrupting' normal text conventions, or 'deviating' from a standard language. Although it is true that many of the defamiliarizing devices of modern literature do involve breaking the rules, even creating new rules, nevertheless texts can be perfectly regular in the terms of my last chapter and still signify more than their propositions literally state. The fact is that a piece of language in real use is *more than* a text put together by the basic conventions which I introduced in the last chapter: a much richer *discourse* than has emerged so far. The extra structure and extra meanings referred to in the title of this chapter are organizations of language which respond to a text's communicative functions. The structure of discourse, as opposed to the more limited structure of text, reflects the whole complex process of people interacting with one another in live situations and within the structure of social forces. In real communication—written as well as spoken—people are doing more than just transmitting neutral propositions to one another in 'sensibly' formed texts. Their language assumes extra structuration reflecting their personal purposes in communication, their social statuses and relationships, and the nature of the setting within which language is used. A speaker may wish to persuade, to inform, to impress, to justify himself, to bully or attack another person, and so on. These purposes will be expressed in linguistic structure, as also will be the relationship between the speaker and his interlocutor: if speakers are very close and intimate (lovers, siblings) their language will be characteristically different from speech on the same topic between individuals who don't know one another very well, or who occupy disparate social statuses, for example, company director and worker, teacher and pupil. Another influence on the text's further structuring as discourse is the kind of setting in which it is produced and received: a love letter is necessarily different in its discourse structure from a formal lecture, a lecture differs from a face-to-face row, all of them from a newspaper advertisement, and so on. So language *as discourse* expresses, by extra structure, the functions and circumstances of the interactions which it mediates. Looking at language from this perspective, we are entering the area of styles and social meanings. When choices of characteristic discourse structures consistently correlate with similar communicative circumstances, we speak of distinct 'styles' and 'genres'. These generalizations are as applicable outside as within 'literature': it is just as valid to describe the styles of popular newspapers, the genre of the TV advertisement, the stylistic conventions used in official notices, the genre 'letters to the Press', etc., as it is to generalize about the genres of Miltonic sonnet, epic, confessional novel, the styles of Augustan verse, seventeenth-century prose, Imagism, and so on, as literary critics do. Once again, we see that the opposition 'literature: non-literature' beloved of literary critics is unnecessary when the uses of language are regarded in a broad enough perspective.

Leaving stylistic generalizations and their interpretations on one side for a moment, in this chapter I shall offer a more detailed focus on a few sample techniques of extra structure which happen to be important in some styles of modern literary discourse. I shall also introduce two major processes which are regularly involved in adding extra structure to texts in the formation of culturally significant discourses.

The extra meanings of additional structure have already been illustrated in a fragmentary way, from the Pope couplet in the first chapter to some of the examples of textual structure analysed in Chapter 5. In the Pope, a social criticism was voiced not by the propositions in the text but by the formal arrangement of the verse which placed 'husbands' and 'lapdogs' in metrically parallel positions, implying their semantic equivalence. *Parallelism and equivalence* is one of the two processes to be explained here. The other is *foregrounding*: whenever some item or construction appears in a text with unusual or noticeable frequency and apparently for some valid reason, then cumulatively a distinctive effect emerges. Examples of foregrounding cited so far would include the highlighted tentative modalities—the 'maybes' —of *Something Happened!* (p. 57 above); the adjective-noun combinations in Akenside (p. 51); the collocating vocabulary of religious ceremony in the opening of *Ulysses* (p. 65). Note that parallelism may be an instance of foregrounding: it is so in Pope, in fact, since it is a constant, and constantly significant, feature of his metrical discourse.

The importance of foregrounding and parallelism has been

argued in two extremely famous and influential articles, by the Prague School poetic theorist Jan Mukařovský and the founder of modern linguistic poetics, Roman Jakobson.[1] These theorists are in the tradition of the Russian formalist school; specifically, both of their proposals can be seen as demonstrations of how language in literature is structured to 'impede' and 'prolong' perception to produce the dehabitualized response described by Shklovksy (see p. 40 above). Although the insights of Mukařovský and Jakobson are profound and constructive, I must immediately dissociate myself from the general aim of their argument: they claim that foregrounding and parallelism are special qualities of 'poetic language' which distinguish it from 'ordinary language'; I maintain that 'poetic language' is not an objective, distinct entity, but an imaginary concept produced by the business of letters by way of publishing, reviewing, criticizing, theorizing and teaching.

For me, foregrounding and parallelism are bases for a number of linguistic techniques through which texts are made into discourses. It happens that certain dominant styles in modern literature depend heavily on these techniques. But other types of discourse use them extensively, for example, advertising, political oratory, rules and regulations, courtroom interrogation, and many others.

*Foregrounding* uses a visual metaphor to explain a linguistic technique. In painting, this would be any device—contrast of hue or lightness, greater detail or linear precision, manipulation of perspective, paint texture or whatever—which causes some part of a composition to be perceived as standing out as a figure against a less determinate background. What is foregrounded in language? According to Mukařovský:

In poetic language foregrounding achieves maximum intensity to the extent of pushing communication into the background as the objective of expression and of being used for its own sake; it is not used in the services of communication, but in order *to place in the foreground the act of expression, the act of speech itself.*

Jakobson's assertions about 'the poetic function of language' are very much in agreement with the part of the Mukařovský statement that I have italicized:

The set (*Einstellung*) toward the MESSAGE as such, focus on the message for its own sake, is the POETIC function of language . . . This function, by promoting the palpability of signs, deepens the fundamental dichotomy of signs and objects. [Jakobson's italics and capitals].

For both of these writers, literary language draws the reader's attention to its own artifices of construction—cohesion or collocation, say, does not function merely as an aid to communication but under foregrounding becomes itself a pattern for independent notice. Signs become palpable, while the objects they designate are backgrounded into subordinate importance. The medium becomes more prominent than the meaning, and that—on the Mukařovský-Jakobson theory—is the reverse of the priorities of ordinary communication.

In my theory, defamiliarizing communication, whether or not it is called 'literature', is discourse in which certain textual structures (of numberless variety) have been made salient by unusual regularity (foregrounded). It is extremely difficult to give any general rules as to what level of repetition and recurrence of structures gives rise to foregrounding, since whether a particular construction is perceived as salient depends on the discourse context in which it appears. For instance, an exceptional number of passives is found in scientific writing, but in that context it is conventional and not noticeable. In the telling of a story, however, even a few passives instead of active sentences are likely to be experienced as an oddity because readers of narrative assume that the essence of the genre is a sequence of actions. I shall not carry these speculations about quantity of foregrounding any further, but let my examples and my readers' intuitions provide further materials for consideration.

As for the motives and functions of foregrounding, the perceptual salience it produces is not, despite our authorities, physical prominence of the expressive medium for its own sake, but extra discourse structure inviting *interpretation*. The significance is additional to the propositional meaning, and often at odds with the latter—as in the Pope example, which speaks of the extremity of grief but implicates the insincerity of those who give vent to it.[2] Once again, the interpretation of foregrounding is easier to grasp through examples than to discuss abstractly.

Mukařovský's 'foregrounding' may be seen as a clarification of Shklovsky's 'impeding perception' in that it suggests that what intervenes between reading and knowledge is a complication of linguistic technique. Jakobson goes a stage further towards specifying exactly what is involved at the level of linguistic structure. For simplicity I have referred to his discovery as 'parallelism and equivalence', but he phrases it in a more careful, complex and only apparently cryptic fashion:

What is the empirical linguistic criterion of the poetic function? In particular, what is the indispensable feature inherent in any piece of poetry? To answer this question we must recall the two basic modes of arrangement used in verbal behavior, *selection* and *combination*. If 'child' is the topic of the message, the speaker selects one among the extant, more or less similar, nouns like child, kid, youngster, tot, all of them equivalent in a certain respect, and then, to comment on this topic, he may select one of the semantically cognate verbs—sleeps, dozes, nods, naps. Both chosen words combine in the speech chain. The selection is produced on the base of equivalence, similarity and dissimilarity, synonymity and antonymity, while the combination, the build up of the sequence, is based on contiguity. *The poetic function projects the principle of equivalence from the axis of selection into the axis of combination.* Equivalence is promoted to the constitutive device of the sequence. In poetry one syllable is equalized with any other syllable of the same sequence; word stress is assumed to equal word stress, as unstress equals unstress; prosodic long is matched with long, and short with short; word boundary equals word boundary, no boundary equals no boundary; syntactic pause equals syntactic pause, no pause equals no pause. Syllables are converted into units of measure, and so are morae or stresses.

Let us give Jakobson's 'axes' their more usual, and more memorable, names. The axis of selection is the *paradigm*; that of combination, the *syntagm*. The syntagm is simply the linear ordering of sounds and of words constructing a sentence 'left-to-right' as it were; the 'horizontal' dimension of the text. A sentence is one kind of syntagm: 'The child sleeps' is a grammatical sequence of an article plus a noun followed by a verb, or from another analytic perspective a subject followed by a predicate, and from another, a sequence of three lexical items 'the' and 'child' and 'sleeps'. This is also a phonological syntagm: a series of three syllables, the first lightly stressed and the second and third more heavily. A more detailed syntagmatic analysis at the level of phonology would show that each word or syllable is a sequence of phonemes arranged according to the phonological conventions of English: /slips/, etc.†

If syntagms are sequences of linguistic elements in actual bits of language, paradigms are the sets of possibilities from which these elements are selected. At each point in the syntagmatic chain, there is a 'vertical' paradigm of other possibilities that might have been selected:

SYNTAGM

| P | The | child | sleeps |
|---|-----|-------|--------|
| A | a | kid | dozes |
| R | some | youngster | nods |
| A | etc. | tot | naps |
| D | | infant | wakes |
| I | | boy | dreams |
| G | | woman | etc. |
| M | | etc. | |

The above paradigms will permit the alternative syntagms 'The kid dozes', 'A woman dreams', etc. The same principle works in phonology: /slips/, /blips/, /slups/, /slaps/, /slaks/, /blaks/, etc. Note that paradigms, being potential resources and not actual pieces of language, are normally 'invisible'—except in grammar books and, on Jakobson's theory, in poems.

By 'equivalent' Jakobson simply means 'substitutable in the same place in a syntagm'; *not* 'identical' or 'synonymous': so not only 'kid' and 'child' are equivalent in his sense, but also opposites or semantically incompatible terms like 'black' and 'white', or 'hot' and 'cold', or 'dove' and 'hawk'. Equivalence includes contrast and other types of paradigmatic relationships.

Jakobson's 'poetic principle' is a kind of foregrounding which includes a vast range of rhetorical techniques, from metrical structure to syntactic parallelism to the semantics of paradox. Its working is very simple. Two or more linguistic units, of whatever kind, which have some paradigmatic relationship, are placed in the sequence of the text in such a way that this relationship is

---

† */tlips/ would not be an acceptable English sequence of phonemes any more than *'sleeps child the' would be accepted as a good syntactic syntagm in the language. Note the use of / / to enclose phonemic transcriptions and of * to indicate an unacceptable sequence at any linguistic level. These are standard notational conventions in linguistics.

clearly perceptible in addition to whatever syntagmatic relationship the items may have. In this way an extra layer of structure is
created over and above the structure of the text as 'sensible communication'. One of Jakobson's examples is the campaign slogan
'I like Ike' /ai laik aik/. Here the principle of phonetic equivalence is carried almost to its limits: each word is only one syllable
long, every vowel is /ai/, the second and third syllables end in
/k/, and every syllable is strongly stressed. None of these equivalences is required by the meanings of the words or by their syntactic relationships. There is a level of phonetic patterning which
is entirely independent of the sentence as *text*. This may seem a
trivial example, but its significance is in principle the same as that
of the more complex cases I will discuss. Anyone familiar with
discourse patterns in English is likely to feel that the matching of
vowels and consonants means something in addition to what is
stated by the sentence—perhaps, the inherent likeability of Ike,
or the inevitability of 'I' liking him. The foregrounded sounds are
not just a palpable musical texture; they are also an invitation to
make meaning.

Jakobson's theory provides (among other things) the basic
recipe for the metrical structure of verse. Most English verse is
constructed on two assumptions of phonetic equivalence. First, a
line consists of a fixed number of syllables, the exact number
varying with the verse type but in the dominant decasyllabic type
of Shakespeare, Milton, Wordsworth, and other major poets,
ten syllables. Thus all successive sequences of ten syllables are
assumed to be 'equivalent' in Jakobson's sense. To achieve these
groupings into tens, syntax has to be carefully arranged, with a
fair proportion of major syntactic boundaries (between sentences
or clauses or phrases) falling at the tenth syllable. Rhymed verse
reinforces the line-endings by extra equivalences—chiming syllables—at those points. The second major structural device in conventional English verse is regularity in the number of strongly
stressed, or prominent, syllables per line, and in the number of
lightly stressed syllables between the prominent ones. In English,
different syntactic classes of word carry different levels of prominence, and within a single word, one syllable will be more prominent than others: for instance, the words 'in', 'and', 'of', and 'a'
in this sentence are less strongly stressed than 'English', 'different', 'prominence', etc; and the words 'different', 'syllable',

'prominent', and others always have the strongest stress on the first syllable. Within the verse line, a sequence of words is selected which, conforming to these stress rules of English, disposes the syllables in their expected metrical positions:

> Not lóuder Shríeks to pítying Héav'n are cást

Variants on an established pattern are frequent; when they occur, they are felt to be significant, at least for setting the characteristic personal metrical style of a particular poet, and often for creating specific reorientations of meaning:

> When Húsbands or when Láp-dogs bréathe their lást

Pope's declining the opportunity to stress the fourth syllable of the line ('or') throws the two focal words 'husbands' and 'lapdogs' into a clear syntagmatic parallelism—with what semantic effect we have already observed but can now explain by application of the Jakobsonian principle: the syntagmatic parallel between the two words invites us to seek a paradigmatic relationship betwen them, to regard them as equivalent in meaning. Metrical structure, we see, is not an independent, decorative, formal pattern but a discourse convention bringing extra meanings to a text.[3]

Let us look at the interaction between the foregrounded parallelism of metre and equivalence at other levels of language in a complete text. William Blake's 'London' (1794) offers a particularly clear example:

> I wander thro' each charter'd street,
> Near where the charter'd Thames does flow.
> And mark in every face I meet
> Marks of weakness, marks of woe.
>
> In every cry of every Man,
> In every Infant's cry of fear,
> In every voice: in every ban,
> The mind-forg'd manacles I hear.
>
> How the Chimney-sweeper's cry
> Every blackning Church appalls,
> And the hapless Soldier's sigh,
> Runs in blood down Palace walls
>
> But most thro' midnight streets I hear
> How the youthful Harlot's curse

Blasts the new-born Infant's tear
And blights with plagues the Marriage hearse.

The repetitions, parallels, and antitheses of this poem can be attributed in part to a metrical motive: constructing one of the childish ballad-like or hymn-like verse rhythms that Blake uses in 'Songs of Innocence' and 'Songs of Experience'. Thus repetitions like 'Marks of weakness, marks of woe' and 'In every . . . in every . . . in every . . . in every' obviously enhance the regularity of the rhythm—and, incidentally, restrict the vocabulary too, so apparently simplifying the style. But any appearance of simplicity of meaning is illusory. The extra formal symmetries of the text draw attention to the lexical paradigms that are displayed in the poem, and call upon us to interpret the relationships between members of these paradigms, to produce complexities of meaning which, judging from the extremely complicated, virtually contradictory, phrase 'Marriage hearse' which ends the poem, are not accidental. Consider line 4:

Marks of weakness, marks of woe.

Here there is syntactic equivalence between the two phrases, identity of the two first words, alliteration of /m/ and of /w/. The conventions of verse discourse encourage the reader to look for a relationship between the matched but different items, 'weakness' and 'woe'. These words have two quite different meanings, are only loosely linked syntactically (both objects of the verb 'mark' in the preceding line), but the parallelism implies a closer relationship. In itself, 'weakness' is a double-valued word: weakness is either pitiable or culpable, depending on one's viewpoint. I suggest that the parallel with 'woe' resolves the value of 'weakness' as 'pitiable' which is of course consistent with the general ethical perspective of the whole poem. And it is by processes such as this that that perspective is built up; not by overt statement.

One foregrounded paradigm is the vocabulary for the vocal laments and exclamations of the pitiable people whom Blake's speaker encounters: 'cry', 'cry of fear', 'voice', 'ban', 'cry', 'sigh', 'curse'. The prominence of these cries, by the mere frequency of the terms, hardly needs comment. It might be asked whether this is a naturalistic picture of a street scene, with the first 'cry' (line 5) referring to someone crying his wares, the 'ban' a public proclamation, and so on. But the distinctness of the cries

seems less remarkable than the way they merge and their meanings develop: the neutral 'cry' accumulates overtones first of pain
and suffering and then rage and malediction. The complex values
of the 'cry' paradigm make sense in the context of the last two
stanzas. The sentences about the chimney-sweep, the soldier and
the harlot are syntactically difficult but their general sense is
clear: the sufferings of these exploited people are a public indictment of the legitimated forces of oppression—religion, monarchy (or, less specifically, state power), and marriage. Syntactic
and metrical parallelisms encourage this interpretation: lines 9,
11 and 14 are syntactically equivalent, as are 10, 12, 15 and 16, so
that their central lexical items are placed in a symmetrical set of
oppositions:

Chimney-sweeper : Church
Soldier: Palace
Harlot: $\begin{cases} \text{Infant} \\ \text{Marriage hearse} \end{cases}$

It is implied that these are antagonistic relationships, and contradictory ones: it is a paradox that the Church, claimed source of
spiritual comfort, is part of the set of economic forces which, to
sustain their power and privilege, subject children to degrading
and dangerous employment. The powerful contradiction 'marriage hearse' has a similar interpretation: the institution of marriage is one part of a sexual institution which also contains child
prostitution as an integral part, and in which the production of
children is as appalling an outcome as the transmission of sexual
diseases. This contradiction 'marriage = death' is only one of
several which emerge when one realizes that ironic paradox is a
strategy of this discourse. At the beginning of the poem, the
repetition 'charter'd street', 'charter'd Thames', might go
unnoticed on a first reading, might be accepted as merely an
ingredient in the sing-song rhythm. A chartered street is
presumably a street whose residents have been granted some
privilege; the privilege is recorded in a document, a charter. Can a
river be chartered in this sense? Hardly, since a river is a natural
but inanimate force not properly under man's control. Society's
claim to charter the Thames is arrogant presumption. If we think
about the meaning of the word 'charter'd' in these terms, the
presumption reflects back on 'charter'd street' as well, and we are

bound to consider what is involved in the granting of privilege by authority. The paradox is of course that a freedom which is officially *licenced* is no freedom at all, and that is a version of the paradox that runs through the whole poem: the oppression of the individual by an apparently benevolent official society. This is nowhere stated in the poem, but will be clear to any experienced reader of verse who understands the paradigmatic relationships foregrounded in the structure of the poem.

This process of reinterpreting the syntagm by foregrounding paradigms works in prose as well as verse. In an illuminating discussion of D. H. Lawrence's story 'The Blind Man', Anne Cluysenaar points out that the parallelism in the first paragraph leads the reader 'to suppose that Isabel favours Bertie over her husband'.[4]

Isabel Pervin was listening for two sounds—for the sound of wheels on the drive outside and for the noise of her husband's footsteps in the hall. Her dearest and oldest friend, a man who seemed almost indispensable to her living, would drive up in the rainy dusk of the closing November day. The trap had gone to fetch him from the station. And her husband, who had been blinded in Flanders, and who had a disfiguring mark on his brow, would be coming in from the out-houses.

Cluysenaar displays the parallelism but, though her interpretation is doubtless correct, she does not explain how it produces the evaluation.

This is the very opening of the story, and the sentences are first and foremost narrative sentences, identifying the main participants and setting the scene. At the level of discourse structure, however, the syntactic parallels of phrase and clause say much more. Note that in each of the paired phrases below, 1 refers to Isabel's friend, Bertie, and 2 to her husband, Maurice:

Isabel Pervin was listening for two sounds—

1. for the sound of wheels . . .
2. and for the noise of her husband's footsteps

'Sound' and 'noise' are near-synonyms from the same lexical paradigm, but the first is neutral as to evaluation, the second negative—noises are unpleasant. This is the origin of the hinted negative evaluation of Maurice. The system of oppositions henceforth depends on conventional cultural associations and the way we relate them to the characters. 'Wheels' connotes mobility, 'footsteps' the limitations of man unassisted by the technology of travel.

1. on the drive outside
2. in the hall

The drive means access to the wide world outside, travel etc., and fits with Isabel's cultivated and cosmopolitan background; the hall connotes containment, the restrictions of domestic life perhaps.

1. Her dearest and oldest friend
2. and her husband

The paradigm 'friend/husband' is introduced oddly here, the friend being both mentioned first and hyperbolized, and the husband referred to second and neutrally, implicitly reducing the status of the husband; the opposition is immediately continued:

1. a man who seemed almost indispensable to her living
2. who had been blinded in Flanders, and who had a disfiguring mark on his brow

Readers who bring to the text conventional assumptions about marriage and its emotional exclusivity must find the 'friend/ husband' paradigm unnaturally inverted. Prospectively, this inversion is disturbing in the light of the following paragraph in which Lawrence has Isabel reflecting on the intensely satisfying and private intimacy of her marriage with Maurice.

1. would drive up . . . from the station
2. would be coming in from the out-houses.

The same opposition as before: with Bertie is associated travel, mobility, the world at large; with Maurice, the meaner parts of the farm buildings (Isabel's fear of and distaste for the farm are quite evident later). In the general terms which might be used by anthropologists, Bertie is analysed as a representative of *culture*, Maurice represents the other term in this powerful opposition, *nature*.

Through various subtle hints, we are told that these evaluations are in Isabel's consciousness: it is she who is named right at the beginning; she is given a verb of active perception, 'was

listening for'; the other characters are introduced in relation to
her rather than as individuals—'her husband', 'her friend'. The
internal perspective[5] is confirmed by the mixed tenses of the first
sentence of the next paragraph—'now' in a past tense sentence
conventionally signals entry into a character's consciousness—
and by the existence of many sentences in a style which could
reasonably represent Isabel's reflective thoughts. But there is
much in this continuation which indicates a troubled and complex perspective:

He had been home for a year now. He was totally blind. Yet they had
been very happy. The Grange was Maurice's own place. The back was a
farmstead, and the Wernhams, who occupied the rear premises, acted as
farmers. Isabel lived with her husband in the handsome rooms in front.
She and he had been almost entirely alone together since he was
wounded. They talked and sang and read together in a wonderful and
unspeakable intimacy. Then she reviewed books for a Scottish newspaper, carrying on her old interest, and he occupied himself a good deal
with the farm. Sightless, he could still discuss everything with Wernham,
and he could also do a good deal of work about the place—menial work,
it is true, but it gave him satisfaction. He milked the cows, carried in the
pails, turned the separator, attended to the pigs and horses. Life was still
very full and strangely serene for the blind man, peaceful with the almost
incomprehensible peace of immediate contact in darkness. With his wife
he had a whole world, rich and real and invisible.

They were newly and remotely happy. He did not even regret the loss
of his sight in these times of dark, palpable joy. A certain exultance
swelled his soul.

Foregrounded here is a vocabulary of *extremes*—extremes of
sensation or emotion or evaluation:

totally blind, very happy, handsome, entirely alone, wonderful,
unspeakable, intimacy, a good deal, everything, very full, strangely,
incomprehensible, immediate, whole world, rich, real, invisible,
remotely, happy, joy, exultance, swelled, soul.

Most of these words and phrases are positive, including, of
course, 'entirely alone' in this context. The general message given
by these judgements is that the Pervins' marriage is exceptionally
happy, that they are intensely and exclusively in love. However,
the foregrounding is so dense that it might be felt to be an overstatement—a symptom that the love is less solid than is claimed.
What is more, some of the words—'unspeakable' for instance—

are potentially negative in their connotations once one concedes the possible insincerity of the context. That has already been hinted in the opening paragraph with its suggestion that Isabel's love for her husband is less secure than her affection for her old friend. And it is explicitly confirmed in the fourth paragraph, which speaks of Maurice's 'devastating fits of depression', and Isabel's consequent dread and sense of burden. So this overblown, hyperbolic, vulnerable language seems justified by the narrative situation.

(There is, however, a radical problem with this technique in Lawrence, namely that he foregrounds the vocabulary of sensation and evaluation indiscriminately, not differentiating the diction according to particular characters' points of view, and often intruding his own judgements into characters' thoughts: the language in which Isabel's thoughts are put is at times violent and out of character; for example, she attributes 'stupid hatred' to her husband. This compositional defect is beyond the scope of the present chapter, but I believe it could be approached through the analysis of foregrounded lexical paradigms.)

## Notes

1. Jan Mukařovský, 'Standard Language and Poetic Language', in Paul L. Garvin, trans., *A Prague School Reader on Esthetics, Literary Structure, and Style* (Washington, DC: Georgetown University Press, 1964), pp. 17–30; Roman Jakobson, 'Closing Statement: Linguistics and Poetics', in Thomas A. Sebeok, ed., *Style in Language* (Cambridge, Mass.: MIT Press, 1960), pp. 350–77. Both papers have been extensively anthologized.
2. This antagonism between two levels of meaning, so common in modern western literature, explains the preoccupation with irony and paradox among literary critics such as Cleanth Brooks, William Empson, and others.
3. Obviously I have made no attempt to give a complete linguistic account of metre, but the subject has been extensively treated elsewhere. See S. Chatman, *A Theory of Meter* (The Hague: Mouton, 1965); M. Halle and S. J. Keyser, *English Stress: Its Form, its Growth, and its Role in Verse* (New York: Harper and Row, 1971); W. K. Wimsatt, ed., *Versification: Major Language Types* (New York: New York University Press, 1972); R. Fowler, 'What is Metrical Analysis?' *Anglia*, 86 (1968), 280–320, reprinted in Fowler, *The Languages of Literature* (London: Routledge and Kegan Paul, 1971), Ch. 10.

4. Anne Cluysenaar, *Introduction to Literary Stylistics* (London: Batsford, 1976), p. 96.
5. On internal perspective see Chapter 9 below and, for more details of the linguistic constructions associated with it, my *Linguistics and the Novel* (London: Methuen, 1977), pp. 89–113.

# 7
# Text and Context

In the previous two chapters I discussed the coherence of texts, the various 'cohesive' constructions for tying sentences together into well-formed wholes; also the semantic implications of cohesion and of some deviations from and additions to regular conventions of cohesive patterning. Textual structure is of great importance in the traditions of verse literature with which readers and teachers in our culture are mainly preoccupied and also in rhetorical prose writing such as the Lawrence passage which we examined in the last chapter: such writers constantly foreground the 'mechanics' of their compositions, the basic constructional devices. By doing this (whether through parallelism, foregrounded collocation, or however) writers produce extra levels of meaning over and above the meanings of the component sentences —often, meanings which are in ironic tension with sentence-meanings, as we have seen, and thus defamiliarizing.

Important as textual patterning is, it is only one part of the structure and process of linguistic communication—and a linguistic criticism which attends exclusively to this part has its limitations. We must now add more dimensions of structure to our linguistic model, and hopefully more strings to our critical bow. For instance, we must look again at the structures and meanings of sentences in themselves, as distinct from their relationships in texts (Chapter 10). Before doing so, however, there is much to say about the dynamics of texts as *interpersonal* communication in contexts, and this will take us well beyond consideration of texts as formal objects.

It is customary to indicate the change of perspective at this point in the argument by distinguishing between 'text' and 'discourse'—a distinction for which we prepared in the previous chapter. To look at language as text entails the study of whole units of communication seen as coherent syntactic and semantic structures which can be spoken or written down. Roughly speaking, texts can be regarded as the *medium* of discourse (remembering of course that in the literary traditions from which I have drawn my examples so far, the medium is given a high-lighted substantiality). Discourse is the whole complicated process of linguistic interaction between people uttering and comprehending texts. To study language as discourse requires, therefore, attention to facets of structure which relate to the participants in communication, the actions they perform through uttering texts, and the contexts within which discourse is conducted. All of these 'extra-linguistic' factors are systematically reflected in the structures of the sentences (and thus texts) which speakers utter. Or, to put it the other way around, the form of language has developed in response to its discourse functions so as to provide the means of expression for all the personal actions, interpersonal relationships, and connections with context that are mediated through discourse.

*Context* is mentioned frequently in literary theory, if only nega-tively: literary works are said to be free of any context, or, alter-natively, to 'create their own contexts'. Therein, it is claimed, lies the difference between literature and 'ordinary discourse'. There is a cluster of differences at issue here, including predominantly the fictionality of literature and also its alleged static or non-kinetic quality, that is to say its alleged failure to excite readers to practical action in the real world. These claims involve quite complicated and abstract problems; before we can judge their validity, we need to clarify what we mean by 'context'. At least three useful meanings can be distinguished, all of them relevant to our present discussion: *context of utterance*, *context of cul-ture*, and *context of reference*.

In the first place there is the immediate *context of utterance*, the situation within which discourse is conducted. This com-prises: the physical surroundings; the location of the participants *vis-à-vis* one another, whether they are two people talking face-to-face, one person addressing a large audience, two people speaking by telephone, a group of informal conversationalists scattered through a large room, or whatever; the channel employed, in particular whether speech or writing. It might seem that contexts of utterance vary in character almost as widely as the number of occasions of utterances, that is, indefinitely. However, human communication is not as random as that, and contexts of utterance tend to fall into types. For a start, there is a fundamental distinction between contexts in which participants are together at the same time and in the same place, and all 'split' contexts of utterance: for example, telephone, or live broadcast, in which the message is produced and received (virtually) simultaneously but in different locations; letters, written and received at different points in space and in time—as is the case with most written or printed communications. Whether, and how, the context of utterance is 'split' has a profound influence on what deictics of time and place can be used (see pp. 57–9 above) and on what they mean: consider, for instance, the different selections and meanings for words like 'here' and 'now' in face-to-face discourse and in a telephone conversation—basic words for locating a discourse in context, but used quite differently according to differences of contextual type. A second systematic difference between types of utterance context involves personal deictics— 'I', 'you', etc.—following a distinction between contexts in which the participants are identifiable individuals and those in which they are not. On the one hand we have Mary Smith talking to Fred Smith; on the other, an unidentified 'I' speaking as the narrator in a nineteenth-century novel or a Renaissance love-poem—not the author speaking in his own voice—addressing an unknown mass readership or a pretended mistress respectively. In the case of the Smiths, the 'I' and the 'you' are real, whereas in the novel and the poem they are imagined and constructed. The latter type of utterance context is highly characteristic of literary texts; I will discuss how the fictional 'I' and 'we' are constructed below.

A third point needs to be made about the regularities of contexts of utterance. Although every utterance (or reception thereof) is a distinct historical event with its own idiosyncracies, there are strong and recognizable recurrent features which group distinct utterance contexts under clear types. These classifying recurrences are the consequences of cultural conventions which sort the objects and activities of societies into categories with their distinct significances. I discussed this process of cultural categorization in Chapter 2, suggesting that it is an essential device for simplifying and making recognizable the material and social world, and that language plays an important part in stabilizing the categories. As far as contexts of utterance are concerned, the settings and participants come to be recognized as stereotypes. The places where discourse occurs are perceived not as individual sites but as instances of institutions or routine settings like 'church', 'classroom', 'sitting room', 'TV studio', etc. As for people, they communicate not just as individuals but in accordance with ascribed roles and statuses deriving from their functions within social structure: 'clergyman', 'teacher', 'child', 'salesman', 'boss', and so on. People's behaviour is strongly affected by their roles and those of others, and by the conventions imposed by settings—and this conventionality of behaviour is characteristic of apparently intimate and informal contexts as well as of more rigid and ceremonial settings. There is ample evidence in the writings of socio-linguists and discourse analysts[1] that the structure of verbal behaviour differs predictably from one type of utterance context to another, and that these variations can be attributed to social and economic factors which extend beyond the immediate setting to the broader structure of society.

Thus our first sense of the word 'context', *context of utterance*, needs to be related to a second sense, *context of culture*: the whole network of social and economic conventions and institutions constituting the culture at large, especially in so far as these bear on particular utterance contexts and influence the structure of discourse occurring within them. The distinction is an important one, particularly in the light of literary–critical discussions which define fictionality as lack of context or unreality of context. It may be plausible to say that the context of *utterance* is peculiar in some literary genres (for example, the Renaissance love-poems already mentioned, or Keats's *Odes*); but all discourse has a definite context of *culture* which may—I would say 'ought to'—be studied as an influence on the linguistic structure of literary texts and as a guide to their interpretation. The relationships between literary discourse and cultural contexts are referred to informally throughout this book.

So far I have discussed two kinds of context which influence the structure of discourse: the immediate, but nevertheless conventional, context of utterance, and the broader, highly structured, context of culture, which may be seen as determining the possible types of utterance contexts—and thus, indirectly but substantially, influencing the kind of discourse which may be used on specific occasions. The third context is what I shall call *context of reference*: the topic or subject-matter of a text. Now one of the most remarkable features of human language, distinguishing it from other animal communication systems, is the relative independence of subject-matter from the contexts of utterance and of culture. The first of these freedoms, often called *displacement*, is the capacity of human speech to refer to things and events removed in space and time from the immediate context of utterance. Whereas the calls of animals and the speech of infants relate to the directly present circumstances of utterance, fully developed human language characteristically refers to contexts outside the here-and-now. The context of reference and the context of utterance do coincide when language is being used to demonstrate or comment on some present activity or object: explaining the controls of a new car—'This is the indicator switch'; commentary on one's own actions—'I'm now approaching the suspect'; cooking or chemistry demonstrations—'Add the contents of this jar to this one'. More often, however (and almost always in written discourse), discourse concerns displaced contexts: narrative, generalization, and prediction, for instance, all involve remote contexts of reference. It can be readily seen that displacement is a prerequisite for narrative and fictional discourse; and that both are entirely natural linguistic practices.

Finally I must mention the relationship between context of reference and context of culture. Once more, there are various possibilities. Non-fictional discourse refers to any individual entities and activities which are both familiar and known to exist within the society referred to by the text. Fictional discourse may refer to such entities, but also adds references to imaginary individuals and events which have not existed (or it is immaterial whether or not they existed). Now these fictional creations may be more or less compatible with the norms of the context of culture. At one extreme we have, for instance, the classic nineteenth-century realist novels, the works of Balzac, George Eliot, Flaubert, Hardy, Zola, in which the fictional world is constructed to approximate closely to a known cultural context. Defamiliarization occurs when the context of reference introduces elements which in any way deviate from the expected cultural context. There are numerous techniques by which this can be effected. They include, for example, the introduction of socio-logically deviant characters with discourse styles at odds with the norms of the narrative voice (the circus people in Dickens's *Hard Times*); children, idiots, and primitives whose world-views are defective or skewed compared with ours; in animal fantasies such as *Watership Down* or *Animal Farm*, the appropriation of 'our' context of culture by beings who are not normally thought to enjoy it; in science fiction, or fantasies such as *The Faerie Queene* or *Gulliver's Travels*, the creation of contexts of reference which are systematic transformations of our world—possible worlds understandable on the basis of our ideology and technology, but not factually experienced, including, for example, beings with brains and motives like ours but dissimilar bodies, or the other way around; finally, there are texts in which the poet attempts to construct a world which is a logical denial or inversion of the experiential norms supplied by the context of culture.

Let us now explore further how deictic and interpersonal features of language are used to construct contexts of utterance and of reference in a number of printed texts. All are 'unnatural' in one way or another, in each case implying a speech situation markedly different from the normal conventions of print. How-ever, I assume that experienced readers of poetry and stories develop ways of accommodating the context of utterance, of naturalizing it while knowing that it is an artefact.

Very many of Yeats's poems begin with, or contain, the first-person deictic pronoun 'I'. A considerable number of these refer to events in Yeats's personal life, or to political issues about which, to our knowledge, he had passionate views, or to aesthetic and philosophical positions to which we know he subscribed. To what extent these poems are autobiographical, or may be said to be Yeats speaking, does not concern us. At least there is the implication that the poems transcribe *a* voice, and in each case it is up to the reader to work out what kind of a speaker this is, in what kind of utterance context: the reader cannot take the literal utterance seriously—Yeats writing fifty years ago, the poems printed, read in 1986—but must construct an artificial context.

Often a title will frame the poem as discourse. The title 'An Irish Airman Foresees his Death' refers to the poem's speaker in the third person, thus indicating the presence of another speaker presenting or quoting the first-person speech in the poem. Note also the verb for a mental process, 'foresees', announcing that the utterance is going to be reflective, not dramatic. The poem opens:

> I know that I shall meet my fate
> Somewhere among the clouds above;

In the sixteen lines of the poem, 'I', 'my' or 'me' appear ten times and there are numerous places where the first-person pronoun must occur in the deep structure but has been deleted:

> I balanced all, [I] brought all to [my] mind

There are a good many third-person references—'Those that I fight' etc.—but no address to any second person ('you'). There are in fact no speech acts such as questions or commands which would involve an addressee in any more active capacity than that of mere 'listener'. The speaker makes a series of assertions, all of them about his own feelings and judgements:

> Those that I fight I do not hate
> Those that I guard I do not love; . . .
>
> A lonely impulse of delight
> Drove to this tumult in the clouds;
> I balanced all, brought all to mind . . .

The discourse is that of an individual reflecting on his own motives and decisions; verbs of thought and sensation abound, from 'know' onwards. It is a context of isolation, as is surely appropriate to the subject-matter: personal rather than interpersonal. Note also that the discourse is scantily provided with deictics of place and time. 'The clouds above' does not mean that the speaker is standing looking up at the sky, nor does 'this tumult in the clouds' imply that he is actually in airborne combat at the time of utterance; helpfully, these two deictic phrases taken together are contradictory, so that we realize they cannot be interpreted literally as referring to the speaker's immediate location but must refer generally to his characteristic activities. As for time reference, that is unfixed: it is psychological, rather than historical. The speaker reflects on his emotions at the moment of speech, recalls the period of decision which led him to assume the situation he is in, speculates on his probable future (death in action) and on the alternative future he has rejected (life with inactivity). The historical background which enabled and inspired Yeats's poem, the service of Robert Gregory in the Royal Flying Corps and his death on 23 January 1918, is a potential context of reference which Yeats has declined to specify in detail within the fictional context of utterance of the poem: the consequence of this choice is that he has produced an effect much admired in poetry, the universal generalizability of an experience which *could* be felt as intensely specific.

Readers may wish to compare the treatment of deixis and reference in a more complicated poem by the same author, 'Among School Children', which I will discuss only briefly. The title and the opening stanza evoke a different kind of utterance context from that of 'An Irish Airman'.

> I walk through the long schoolroom questioning,
> A kind old nun in a white hood replies;
> The children learn to cipher and to sing,
> To study reading-books and history,
> To cut and sew, be neat in everything
> In the best modern way—the children's eyes
> In momentary wonder stare upon
> A sixty year old smiling public man.

Here the printed poem context is more definitely supplanted by the impression of a speaking voice. The crucial difference begins with the present tense action predicate 'walk' contrasted with the mental state 'know' of the other poem. 'Know' implies no determinate point in time; 'I walk' must mean either 'I am now walking' or, less plausibly in this very particularized context of reference, 'I habitually walk'. All the specific details in this stanza suggest a particular scene within which the speaker is walking and commenting on his own actions and the responses of others: the locative expressions 'Among School Children', 'through the long schoolroom'; the particular nun and the expression in the children's eyes; the precise qualifiers 'long', 'white hood', etc.; the report of the nun's speech including a phrase which sounds like her own idiom, 'In the best modern way'. I suggest that this discourse, though printed and necessarily indirect, is constructed to mime not only a spoken context of utterance, but moreover a context of reference which corresponds

to the implied context of utterance. But if you study the corres-
ponding discourse features in the rest of the poem, you will find
that the context of reference shifts away from the implied context
of utterance as the speaker's attention moves away from the
classroom (in which we presume him still to stand) to meditate on
youth, beauty, age, wisdom, and art. The effect of removal from
context is produced not only by esoteric and distant references
('Ledean body', 'Quattrocento', 'Plato') but also by basic discourse features: for instance, the frequency of verbs denoting
thought and other inner processes—stanzas 2–4 begin 'I dream of
a Ledean body', 'And thinking of that fit of grief or rage', and
'Her present image floats into the mind'. The discourse moves
into the contemplative mode of the 'Irish Airman', implying an
isolated thinker who asks rhetorical questions but needs no
respondent—there are no 'you'-involving speech acts.

The dramatic monologue, a form perfected by Browning, aims
to imitate speech in an immediate context of utterance. By an
extreme foregrounding of the interpersonal and deictic parts of
language, the poet creates not only the illusion of a speaking
voice, but also the impression of an addressee towards whom the
voice is projected, and a sense of location and movement within a
physical space. There are no 'stage directions', no dialogue; all
this is done through the utterance of the sole speaker. The opening and closing lines of Browning's 'My Last Duchess' will illustrate the processes which produce these effects. The speaker, an
Italian Duke, talks to an emissary from a Count whose daughter
the Duke intends to marry; the marriage arrangements are to be
discussed, but first the Duke shows the messenger a painting of
his late wife and speaks of his suspicions of her infidelity. The
thirty or so lines which I have omitted from the middle of the
poem give the Duke's account of his Duchess's 'trifling' and of
her punishment by death.

> That's my last Duchess painted on the wall,
> Looking as if she were alive. I call
> That piece a wonder, now: Fra Pandolf's hands
> Worked busily a day, and there she stands.
> Will't please you sit and look at her? I said      5
> 'Fra Pandolf' by design, for never read
> Strangers like you that pictured countenance,
> The depth and passion of its earnest glance,

But to myself they turned (since none puts by
The curtain I have drawn for you, but I)                10
And seemed as they would ask me, if they durst,
How such a glance came there; so, not the first
Are you to turn and ask thus. . . .

                                    There she stands
As if alive. Will't please you rise? We'll meet         15
The company below, then. I repeat,
The Count your master's known munificence
Is ample warrant that no just pretence
Of mine for dowry will be disallowed;
Though his fair daughter's self, as I avowed            20
At starting, is my object. Nay, we'll go
Together down, sir. Notice Neptune, though,
Taming a sea-horse, thought a rarity,
Which Claus of Innsbruck cast in bronze for me!

The poem starts with a deictic (pointing word) 'That's' and contains many others: 'that piece', 'there', etc.; all refer to the portrait of the Duchess, or its position, or some aspect of what is pictured in it. All are distancing deictics, indicating an object at some remove from the speaker (contrast 'this', 'here'). They function to indicate that the speaker and the portrait occupy determinate and related points in space, but no doubt psychological distance is suggested too. The setting is elaborated in a few locative phrases, adverbs, and especially by verbs of placing and movement. Actually, there are few locative adverbs or phrases: 'on the wall', 'below'. The main indicators of space, other than the deictics proper, are verbs of motion or location: 'stands' (twice), 'turn' (twice), 'sit', 'rise', 'go down', plus one or two other verbs which imply change of position, such as 'drawn', 'meet' ( = go to meet). The preponderance of verbs of motion over adverbs of location has the important effect, in this poem in which an inert printed text enacts the speech gestures of a person, of suggesting that the Duke, and the Count's emissary, are interacting dynamically rather than fixed within a statically described scene.

Indicators of time have some importance. The action takes place at a significant 'now': not just the narrative 'now' of a storyteller recollecting the past, but the dramatic 'now' of a wife-murdering Duke, a silent messenger and an absent prospective bride. The ominous relationships between time-spheres are already indicated in the first line with its startling juxtaposition of present and past and its implications of a fateful future. The past tense of 'last' makes it clear that she is *not* alive but present only in a painted image which serves as a warning to 'triflers'; since 'last' in this context means 'previous' and not 'final one of a series', we and the messenger must sense the threat to the future bride.

Moving from deictic to interpersonal features, we notice that as might be expected there is a high density of personal pronouns. 'I' (and variants), referring to the Duke, occurs 19 times in the complete poem; 'you' referring to the messenger 6 times, with another 3 in which 'you' is ambiguously either the messenger or the generalized 'you'—'anyone'; 'we' links the Duke and the messenger twice; 'she' referring to the dead Duchess or her picture occurs 23 times—and there are numerous other noun phrases that refer to her. The frequency of first- and second-person pronouns obviously contributes to the sensation of a face-to-face discourse between persons; the large number of 'I' forms is an index of the Duke's self-importance and potential for tyranny; the 'she' pronouns hint at the strength of his obsession for the woman he has had killed.

Finally, the dramatic tone of the poem is heightened by— among other conversational features of style—the large variety of speech acts indicated by the text. More precisely, there is a large variety of speech acts departing from the neutrality of statements and narrative reports. The poem opens with a demonstrative 'That's' which implies an accompanying gesture. 'I call . . .' is an act of judgement. 'Fra Pandolf's hands . . .' is a narrative report, followed by another demonstrative 'and there she stands'. 'Will't please you . . .' is an indirect command phrased with sham politeness; it recurs at the end of the poem, with other indirect commands—'Nay, we'll go . . .'—and a plain imperative: 'Notice Neptune . . .'. In the body of the narration, the Duke interrupts himself with questions and exclamations: '— how shall I say?—'. Frequently the Duke draws attention to his own acts of speech as if emphasizing the power of his words: 'I call . . .', 'I said . . .', 'I gave commands', 'I repeat . . .', 'as I avowed . . .'. These vocal gestures, essentially alien to the printed page, dramatize the speaker and the scene, and, of course *characterize* him at the same time: authoritarian, indeed tyrannical to the point of committing ducal murder, self-centred, maniacal perhaps in his erratic switches between highly diverse acts of speech.

In discussing these three poems, I have concentrated on ways in which deictic and interpersonal parts of the printed texts suggest three different modes of discourse: a reflective discourse; the speech or thought of a man in a classroom and later withdrawing into his own reflections; and the speech of one person addressing another in direct interaction: in all of these cases, a spoken context of utterance is fictitiously built out of a written text. As we reconstruct the dramatic situation, and begin the activity of interpreting the discourse, we start to draw upon features which relate the language to a context of culture, a social and historical context in which people interact through language which reflects their social roles and statuses. So, for instance, Browning's and our characterization of the Duke depends on assumptions about how power, authority, and manipulation are encoded in English. (Though the context of *reference* is vaguely antique Italian, the linguistically relevant context of *culture* relates to Browning's only slightly archaic English.) We assume, for example, that a polite, modalized invitation spoken by the Duke, a social superior (lines 5 and 15), is not polite and considerate at all, but actually a strong and only hypocritically polite command. We make this assumption on the basis of our knowledge of the way power-relations and language intersect in the socio-linguistic conventions of English, and we constantly bring this sort of socio-linguistic knowledge into play when we reconstruct the cultural meanings of texts.

I shall end this chapter with an example of the importance of socio-linguistic structure, taken from a very familiar play, Shakespeare's *King Lear*. This will, incidentally, illustrate not only the linguistic relevance of context of culture, but also another argument which was introduced at the beginning of this book: the function of linguistic criticism in reactivating for modern readers patterns of language which may have lost their force through historical changes in the language, and/or the familiarity of the literature. In this case, the dramatic power of a scene from a classic play is enhanced if we twentieth-century readers can respond to the social nuances of some sixteenth-century pronoun usages which are no longer current in modern English.

In Act I Scene 2 of the play, the old King Lear is in the process of dividing up his kingdom among his three daughters, Goneril, Regan and Cordelia, in proportion to their professed love to him, which he requires them to declare publicly. Goneril and Regan co-operate with their father, but Cordelia is unwilling to participate in what she seems to regard as an act of emotional blackmail in which her sisters have colluded hypocritically. The Earl of Kent supports her, attacks the king for making this irrational and unfatherly demand; thereby places himself in a state of rebellion against the king, incurs Lear's wrath, and is banished. The text criticizes Lear for giving the formal powers of monarchy expression in an inhuman demand which overrides the personal bonds of family and the loyalty and affection of Kent. One of the ways in which this tension between the personal and the formal is signalled is through the forms of address—names and pronouns —which the characters employ with one another. The linguistic patterns involved are not peculiar to this play, but refer to socio-linguistic conventions which apparently still had some force in Elizabethan English, though probably weakening. The relevant pronoun usages have now disappeared from English, though our language still possesses forms of address which systematically express types of personal relationships. These relationships are clearly encoded in the personal pronoun systems of other modern languages, for instance French and German.[2] The relationships concerned are power and subordination; distance and solidarity or intimacy. Two social equals may indicate their similar status, and the lack of closeness in their personal relationship, by addressing one another as 'Mr Smith', 'Miss Jones', or in French by the pronoun *vous*; an intimate relationship, for example, family or close friends, or a solidary relationship, for example, young people together, may be indicated by mutual *tu* in French, or mutual first names in either language. *In*equality of status, however, selects from the same set of linguistic forms, but the meanings are different in the changed social circumstances. A superior (manager, aristocrat, judge, teacher, etc.) may express power or control over a subordinate by using *tu* or first name, while the person of lower status must reply with *vous* or title alone, or title and last name (*Doctor, Doctor Finlay*). A range of extremely important social meanings is encoded in a very economical set of linguistic forms whose use is subject to severe restrictions, which of course apply more strongly to the inferior of any pair of people. In a tight linguistic system, deviation from the rules is extremely noticeable: for instance, the use of a familiar form such as *tu* or a first name by someone of lower status when addressing someone of higher status makes a potentially suspect and rejectable claim of equality and intimacy. Also, these socio-linguistic systems often contain more meanings than there are terms to express them, so that some utterances are disturbingly ambiguous: for instance, *tu* spoken by someone of high status (A) to someone of lower status (B) may either be an assertion of the power difference and of A's right to condescend to B, or a gesture of solidarity with B. The ambiguity creates unease: why does my doctor call me 'Roger', and can I return his first-name (if I know it)?

These two instabilities—challenge to authority and the nature of a claim to authority—are central to what is happening in the narrative and the thematic development in the scene from *Lear*, and they are expressed and reinforced in the language of address: pronouns, names, and titles. The pronoun system, on which I shall concentrate, is very simple. There are two options (with variants) which one person can use to address another: *thou* (*thee/thy/thine*) and *you* (*your*). They function like *tu* and *vous* in French or *du* and *Sie* in German: *thou* is used either 'downwards' by a superior, in which case it encodes status, or 'sideways', reciprocally, between intimates; *you* is deferential when used 'upwards' by a subordinate (who must not use *thou* in that situation), but is distant if respectful, perhaps neutral, between non-intimates of any rank.

The situation in this scene is formal and serious, and, as we would expect, the address forms begin by following the conventions strictly. Lear marks the ceremonial of the occasion by using the royal *we*:

> Know that we have divided
> In three our Kingdom.                    (37–8)†

He asks his three daughters in turn 'Which of you shall we say doth love us most?' (51) First Goneril replies with the polite,

---

† Line numbers refer to the Arden edition, ed. Kenneth Muir (London: Methuen, 1957).

deferential *you* emphasizing her public, rather than family, relationship with her father:

> Sir, I love you more than word can wield the matter;
> Dearer than eyesight . . .
> Beyond all manner of so much I love you.     (55–61)

Lear responds with the *thou* form:

> Of all these bounds . . .
> We make thee lady: to thine and Albany's issue . . .     (63–7)

Note that it is impossible to tell whether Lear is using the *thou* of condescension or that of family intimacy in this context, but it does not matter because the interaction between the king and his eldest daughter is, from their point of view, proceeding smoothly.

Identical non-reciprocal address (Lear *thou*; Regan *you*) is found in the parallel exchange with the next daughter (67–82). But a shift occurs as Lear moves from Regan ('To thee and thine . . .' 79) to Cordelia ('what can you say . . .?' 85). Cordelia is about to decline to declare how much she loves her father, and Lear's two *you*s (85, 86), by contrast with the *thou* he is entitled to use, and has just used in addressing Goneril and Regan, may show an anticipatory nervousness. For twenty lines, Lear and Cordelia's dialogue employs reciprocal *you* frequently and consistently. Cordelia's *you* is the expected pronoun of deference:

> [I] obey you, love you, and most honour you.     (98)

whereas Lear's *you* suggests distance, the refusal of intimate *thou*:

>                   Mend your speech a little,
> Lest you may mar your fortunes.     (94–5)

Suddenly he shifts to *thou* and begins to use it consistently in addressing Cordelia; in the first instance (105) affectionately as a father, then (108 onwards) harshly and dismissively: his exploitation of the threatening ambiguity of this pronoun is part of the way Shakespeare's text builds up an impression of dangerous capriciousness in his character:

COR. Sure I shall never marry like my sisters,
   To love my father all.

LEAR. But goes thy heart with this?
COR.                                    Ay, my good Lord.                    105
LEAR. So young, and so untender?
COR.  So young, my Lord, and true.
LEAR. Let it be so; thy truth then be thy dower.

After a succession of venomous curses, he concludes by dismiss-
ing her as 'thou my sometime daughter' (120). At this point Kent
tries to intervene on Cordelia's behalf, but he is silenced by Lear
who goes on with his business of dividing his kingdom between
Goneril and Regan, excluding Cordelia. Kent manages to speak
in line 139, and, significantly, attempts to placate Lear by
invoking his own relationships of subordination to the King.
When Lear threatens him again, Kent's language changes completely; in saying that Lear has abdicated his authority as a king
and lost his reason, Kent explicitly announces his personal rebellion by addressing Lear with no less than 16 insubordinate *thou*s
in twenty lines:

KENT.                                    Royal Lear,
    Whom I have ever honour'd as my King,                    140
    Lov'd as my father, as my master follow'd,
    As my great patron thought on in my prayers,—
LEAR. The bow is bent and drawn; make from the shaft.
KENT. Let it fall rather, though the fork invade
    The region of my heart: be Kent unmannerly                    145
    When Lear is mad. What would'st thou do, old man?
    Think'st thou that duty shall have dread to speak
    When power to flattery bows? To plainness honour's bound
    When majesty falls to folly. Reserve thy state;
    And, in thy best consideration, check                    150
    This hideous rashness; answer my life my judgment,
    Thy youngest daughter does not love thee least . . .

These *thou*s are an affront to the King, who in a series of furious
speeches rages against Kent's insolence and finally consigns him
to exile. Naturally, he addresses Kent with *thou*, the *thou* of
contemptuous power. As Kent leaves, he gives Cordelia one intimate *thou*, indicating the affection of an elder who recognizes her
sincerity and has her dearest interests at heart: 'The Gods to their
dear shelter take thee, maid . . .' (182).

    The second-person pronouns are part of a set of interpersonal
linguistic features (including naming and speech acts) which

build up the characterization, narrative, and themes in this early scene of the play. The interpersonal tensions and shifts of behaviour and affiliation which unfold here are very precisely controlled by the structure of the text: Lear's instability, the destructive effects of institutional power (monarchy) obliterating personal allegiances and family obligations; the personalities of the main protagonists as the text constructs and explores them. But it cannot be emphasized too strongly that it is not this particular text alone which by its own unique structure creates the opening position in *King Lear*: rather, it is the relationship between the textual structures and the cultural context which in Elizabethan England, and now, gives the text meaning. The main structures that are active here are interpersonal forms of language, which signify only by virtue of the society's assumptions about how people relate. The cultural context supplies systems of beliefs about the rights and responsibilities of monarchs, parents, subjects, children, their relationships with one another and the ways these relationships are monitored and managed. The audience or reader of the play needs to bring these assumptions to his understanding of the play as its text unfolds, and the text's language (here, pronouns, etc.) instructs the reader towards analysis of and reflection on the values that are at issue in the play.

## Notes

1. See, for instance, P. Trudgill, *Sociolinguistics* (Harmondsworth: Penguin, 1974); P. P. Giglioli, ed., *Language and Social Context* (Harmondsworth: Penguin, 1972); W. Labov, *Sociolinguistic Patterns* (Philadelphia: University of Pennsylvania Press, 1972); D. Hymes, *Foundations in Sociolinguistics* (London: Tavistock, 1977).
2. See R. Brown and A. Gilman, 'The Pronouns of Power and Solidarity', in P. P. Giglioli, ed., *Language and Social Context* (Harmondsworth: Penguin, 1972), pp. 252–82; S. M. Ervin-Tripp, 'Sociolinguistic Rules of Address', in J. B. Pride and J. Holmes, eds., *Sociolinguistics* (Harmondsworth: Penguin, 1972), pp. 225–40.

# 8
# Some Aspects of Dialogue

The previous chapter encourages a view of texts as discourses, as interactions between speakers and addressees real, implied, or fictional. In my opinion this is a most important emphasis, a corrective to the view in literary criticism of texts as objects rather than interactions: as 'verbal icons', 'monuments', or 'well-wrought urns'. The latter phrase is taken from a poem of Donne's by the critic Cleanth Brooks and applied to all poetry: we are meant to recall Keats's silent Grecian Urn, an unspeaking but meaningful artefact. But 'literary' texts, like all texts, *do* speak: they participate in society's communicative practices, and are an important means of influencing world-view and social structure. In this chapter I want to examine some aspects of linguistic structure which concern interaction directly: *dialogic* structures, both in the sense of structures through which fictional characters appear to interact, and in the sense of structures which determine the author's or narrator's relationships with his readers and his characters.

The structure of conversation is very much more complex than that of sentences taken singly, or even cohesive but monologic texts; this complexity is only emerging recently. I cannot explain or illustrate the whole range of conversational features that have been proposed, but will pick out three that seem to be relatively promising: *sequencing*, *speech acts*, and *implicature*.

*Sequencing* is the ordering of contributions to conversations. There are elaborate conventions for arranging the openings, developments and closings of conversations; conventions for holding the floor, interrupting, and turn-taking.[1] They vary according to the setting, the statuses and relationships of the speakers, and the topics of discourse. Who speaks first? What is an appropriate opening move in a particular setting? Given A's first remark, what possibilities are open to B? Must B simply respond with a 'yes' or a 'no' and expect A to carry on controlling the dialogue, or may B assume the stage, begin a new topic and develop it, reserving the initiative to himself? The types of greetings used, the forms of questions asked, even the speed and intonations of contributions, intricately manage the sharing of a conversation between participants. Even a tiny interchange uses structure very precisely to govern what happens, how much is said, and who says it. Take, for instance, the following short telephone call which interrupted my writing of this paragraph:

|   |                                                              |
|---|--------------------------------------------------------------|
|   | 1. ***                                                       |
| A | 2. Hello?                                                    |
| B | 3. (Pause) Hello, is that Roger Fowler?                       |
| A | 4. Yes.                                                      |
| B | 5. Oh it's Ian Jones here; 6. have you got a couple of minutes? |
| A | 7. Yes, sure. (Waits)                                        |
| B | 8. Have you got a couple of minutes in, say, five minutes' time? |
| A | 9. Yes, do you want to come down here?                        |
| B | 10. OK, five minutes.                                        |
| A | 11. See you then, bye-bye.                                   |
| B | 12. Bye-bye.                                                 |

The first move occurs (1) through the ringing of the phone (the type of ring, incidentally, signalling that this is a call from within the University). I respond minimally, not identifying myself (2). The caller does not recognize my voice, pauses and checks my identity (3); notice that he does this through a yes/no question which severely restricts the range of reply options available to me (4). In this way the caller keeps the advantage, reserving his right to begin the informative part of the call. He identifies himself (5) and maintains a high voice pitch level as he moves to a request for my attention (6). Again, this is a yes/no question—to which the answer 'no' would be very difficult! By this time I have identified the caller and guessed that he wishes to tell me something confidential and ask my advice. I wish to get back to my writing as quickly as I can, and the silence labelled 'waits' is intended to tell him to get it off his chest there and then. The caller rejects this move by repeating his wording of (6) in (8), with the additional phrase 'in, say, five minutes' time'. This is an absurd question at face value, so I am obliged to interpret it as a request for a private interview. I, having the status, nominate my office as meeting-place (9); B confirms, indicating, by repetition, insistence (10). There is nothing more to say, so I initiate a farewell sequence (11) which B promptly closes (12).

This conversation worked well partly because the participants know each other and the kind of topics on which they have spoken in the past: even casually acquainted people draw on pre-existing common knowledge to help their conversations proceed smoothly and meaningfully. But in large part, the efficiency stems from the fact that the conversation unfolds according to a plan. I do not mean that the speakers consciously calculate what they are going to say at each point in the dialogue. As usual in language structure, such plans are abstract blueprints known unconsciously. The speakers have confident experience of how such calls proceed, and at each point in the sequence produce types of utterance which progress the conversation in a manner which is appropriate to the type of interaction, and to their relationship and purposes. The Americans Schegloff and Sacks have proposed rules for openings, closings, and sequencings, with particular attention to what they call 'adjacency pairs', interlocked or interdependent consecutive utterances. Sinclair and Coulthard of Birmingham University have proposed a complementary scheme classifying the types of acts and moves performed through smaller and larger parts of conversations. For both types of analysis, see the book by Coulthard cited in note 1 below.

The most important approach to speech as action is the theory of *speech acts* or *illocutionary acts* originally proposed by J. L. Austin, and developed by J. R. Searle.[2] The basic insight is that language-use has an extra dimension which has been somewhat neglected by logicians and linguists: a performative dimension. Those scholars have traditionally been preoccupied with the propositional and semantic functions of language. The linguist is interested in how language encodes meanings, and in such semantic properties as well-formedness, ambiguity, contradiction, tautology, etc.; the logician, in the conditions for the truth or falsehood of the propositions expressed in languages (including the artificial languages of symbolic logic) and in logical relationships between propositions in terms of truth-criteria. Our speech-act philosophers, however, observed that language also has a *pragmatic* function: utterances are used to perform actions as well as to communicate propositions true or false. This principle is easy to grasp in connection with certain utterances containing performative verbs such as *promise, declare, name, baptize, request, order, guarantee*. Consider the sentences:

I promise to pay you five pounds.
I declare this fête open.

A person uttering one of these sentences conveys a proposition about a financial promise or about opening, a fête. But in addition, the utterance of the sentence actually constitutes the action referred to. It is literally a speech act, not just saying something but doing something through speaking. Notice that the logical test of truth doesn't apply in these cases. The criterion for the success of these is not whether they are true but whether they are appropriately uttered. A successful speech act of promising, for instance, requires that several conditions be fulfilled, including that whatever is promised must be a future act of the speaker, that he intends to do it and intends his utterance to commit himself to doing it; that he would not do whatever he promises in the normal course of events (otherwise there would be no point in promising); that he believes the person he is addressing would prefer him to do it ('I promise to burn your house down' would only be a successful promise if we were conspiring to commit an insurance fraud). Presumably all speech acts have their conditions of appropriateness, differing widely from case to case: only marriageable people—not dogs or babies—can be declared man and wife, you cannot consecrate a supermarket, and so on. Defamiliarization can occur if a speech act is spoken in inappropriate circumstances—a deliberate source of verbal comedy, for example: 'I name this cat *The Skylark*.'
Speech acts can be based on constructions other than explicit performative verbs. Instead of saying 'I order you to shut the door' one might say 'Shut the door' or even 'Could you shut the door?' which looks like a question about the addressee's physical ability but in the right conditions is likely to be taken as an *indirect speech act* of ordering. Finally, when we consider that an order may be successfully communicated by an apparently simple descriptive statement 'The door is open', it becomes clear that there is no direct, predictable link between a specific type of linguistic construction and a specific speech act. The important thing to note is the prevalence of speech acts in discourse: the fact that speakers in dialogue continuously engage in a series of illocutionary acts such as requesting, undertaking, challenging, asserting, warning, and so on. This is the chief mechanism by

which conversation is maintained as a practical interaction as well as a channelling of ideas.

The third aspect of dialogue which I want to maintain is important for linguistic criticism is *implicature*: roughly, what is said 'between the lines'. This relates to the traditional notion that one can say one thing and mean something else (for example, irony, metaphor, *double entendre*). Neglected in linguistics until recently, discussed by literary critics with no great clarity, these obscure processes have been studied with insight by the philosopher H. P. Grice, to whom we owe the term 'implicature'.[3] An implicature is a proposition emerging from something that is said, but not actually stated by the words uttered, nor logically derivable from them. It must therefore be a product of the relationship between utterance and context; and a vital part of context would be the knowledge and motives of speaker and addressee. It is in the latter area that Grice's suggestions are most interesting. He suggests that conversation takes place under the guidance of a *co-operative principle* which binds speakers to express themselves in such a way as not to impede interpretation —and hearers to assume that whatever is addressed to them is designed to make sense, so that they make an effort to find an interpretation even when the language does offer difficulties. The speaker's obligations are summarized by Grice under four *maxims*:

1. *Quantity*
    (a) Make your contribution as informative as is required (for the current purposes of the exchange).
    (b) Do not make your contribution more informative than is required.

2. *Quality*
    Try to make your contribution one that is true.
    (a) Do not say what you believe to be false.
    (b) Do not say that for which you lack adequate evidence.

3. *Relation*
    Be relevant.

4. *Manner*
    Be perspicuous.
    (a) Avoid obscurity of expression.
    (b) Avoid ambiguity.
    (c) Be brief.
    (d) Be orderly.

Conversational implicatures characteristically arise when a hearer judges that the speaker has deliberately flouted one of the maxims. Suppose A and B are talking about X, a bank manager who, both agree, is exceptionally tight-fisted when it comes to lending money. A comments: 'He's absolutely the most gener- ous, tolerant manager in the whole history of banking.' A has flouted maxim 2(a) by saying something both A and B agree to be false. A *implicates* the reverse of what he says: he is being iron- ical. What is more, he pads out what he says in excess words and phrases; his hyperbolic expressions—flouting either maxim 1(b) or 4(c)—draw attention to the fact that there is something unstraightforward about the statement, and they invite B to interpret it. And B, the addressee, is bound by his side of the co-operative principle to attempt to make sense of the utterance, so he recovers the implicature.

Although the theory of implicature was expressed by Grice in very informal terms and remains fuzzy in its details, it enriches our view of how discourse works, and promises numerous insights for linguistic criticism. As far as dialogue is concerned, the tech- nique of flouting maxims and raising implicatures is central to dialogic structure in a good deal of elliptical, allusive modern drama such as Pinter's plays; and to dialogue in witty, or ironic, or stylized, novels.[4] My analysis of the Fielding passage, below, could be rethought in terms of implicature, though that is not the terminology I have chosen of this occasion.

(Digressing for a while from the topic of dialogue, there is another important link between the flouting of the maxims and the argument of the present book. As we have seen, writers can deliberately flout the maxims and still make sense, in the know- ledge that their readers have tacitly agreed that deviations are purposeful, intended to provoke a search for meaning. Thus, writers are permitted to say less (Imagism), or say more (Faulkner, Proust) than might be expected (maxim 1); utter what is known to be false or unevidenced (fairy-stories, science fiction) (maxim 2); create unexpected transitions between discrepant sub- jects (Joyce, *nouveau roman*) (maxim 3); be obscure, ambiguous, verbose, disjointed (*Finnegans Wake*, Symbolist poetry, Dylan Thomas) (maxim 4). In 'literary' works such breaches are not just tolerated, but applauded as producing aesthetically or concept- ually agreeable verbal effects. The best book of literary criticism in this century, William Empson's *Seven Types of Ambiguity* (1930), extensively justifies and celebrates breaches of maxim 4(b). I have no doubt that, if the classification of maxims could be made clearer and more discriminating, it would greatly assist the understanding of the traditional 'poetic' figures such as metaphor, metonymy, hyperbole, litotes, etc. This book is not devoted to a detailed survey of poetic figures; but it is worth pointing out a more general link: between the breaching of the maxims and the whole process of defamiliarization.

Breaches of the maxims have exactly the effect that Shklovsky detects in 'artistic' language: they 'make forms difficult . . ., increase the difficulty and length of perception' (p. 41 above). The linguistic peculiarities found in 'literary' texts, like those breaches of the maxims that produce implicatures, are *motivated*: there is a reason for the deviation, and it is up to the reader to figure out that reason; then guided by the structure of the text and its relation to implied context, the reader arrives at a new perspective on what is being expressed. The structures stemming from deviations from the maxims correspond closely to 'literary' figures, and these are, of course, the figures which give rise to defamiliarization.

Many of the defamiliarizing examples quoted earlier in this book can be understood in the light of motivated breaches of specific maxims. Briefly, the description of the Yahoos quoted from *Gulliver's Travels* (p. 43 above) can be explained as a breach of the maxim of quantity, the withholding of the information that these are humans giving less information than might be expected, so producing an ironic surprise when the penny drops. Tolstoy's description of a stage quoted above (p. 42) has the same effect. The opening of *Pride and Prejudice* (p. 57 above) deliberately flouts the maxim of quality for ironic purposes: Jane Austen makes her narrator claim as a truth universally acknowledged a proposition which is manifestly not so. Chandler's detective Marlowe is pointedly inconsequential, flouting a maxim of manner (p. 67). Many more of my examples of defamiliarization can be regarded in the light of the maxims, and readers may care to look at other passages in this book and consider how the maxims might be refined so as to shed a more focused illumination on the techniques of defamiliarization.)

The co-operative principle embodies not just a willingness to be mutually helpful, but an agreement to bring to the comprehension of utterances bodies of shared knowledge (ideology, belief systems, in the terms of Chapters 1–2). That which is implied 'between the lines' may not be created afresh—which is what the theory of implicature and defamiliarization suggests—but may be conventional and expected. In a masterly explication of the implied propositions underpinning a psychotherapeutic interview, Labov and Fanshel have demonstrated how conventional knowledge is an essential element in the interpretation of discourse.[5] Their work may provide a model for thematic criticism. The implicit themes and preoccupations of a text, or an author, or a genre of discourse, or the significance of a particular passage, might be approached by way of a study of recurrent, repeated general propositions. I have tried this informally with *Look Back in Anger*, below, and the extract from *Tom Jones* analysed at the end of this chapter. Questions of shared knowledge are particularly interesting and problematic when, as in our relationship with Fielding, we are trying to decode older works after major ideological shifts have occurred.

Returning from the extension of dialogic concepts to the study of literal dialogue, I want to show how sequencing, speech acts and implicature are deployed to create a verbal illusion of interaction in plays. First, I have chosen the opening of John Osborne's *Look Back in Anger* (1956). Three characters dominate this part of the action: Jimmy Porter, his wife Alison, and their friend and co-lodger, Cliff. In his introductory stage-direction, Osborne speaks of 'the uneasy polyphony of these three people'. Polyphony in music is the simultaneous voicing of several separate musical lines—strands which are not in unison. Certainly, these three characters speak in very distinct tones, and they are often discordant. Much of the dialogue consists of verbal harassment of Alison and Cliff by Jimmy, and their attempts to evade his attacks. Jimmy is outrageous and rude, but not only as an effect of his abusive vocabulary; rather, the whole manipulative strategy of his conversation characterizes him as a destructive, self-pitying, bully.

Here is the text of the opening of the play:

1. JIMMY. Why do I do this every Sunday? Even the book reviews seem to be the same as last week's. Different books—same reviews. Have you finished that one yet?

2. CLIFF. Not yet.
3. J. I've just read three whole columns on the English Novel. Half of it's in French. Do the Sunday papers make *you* feel ignorant?
4. C. Not 'arf.
5. J. Well, you *are* ignorant. You're just a peasant. [*To Alison*] What about you? You're not a peasant are you?
6. ALISON. [*absently*]. What's that?
7. J. I said do the papers make you feel you're not so brilliant after all?
8. A. Oh—I haven't read them yet.
9. J. I didn't ask you that. I said—
10. C. Leave the poor girlie alone. She's busy.
11. J. Well, she can talk, can't she? You can talk, can't you? You can express an opinion. Or does the White Woman's Burden make it impossible to think?
12. A. I'm sorry. I wasn't listening properly.
13. J. You bet you weren't listening. Old Porter talks, and everyone turns over and goes to sleep. And Mrs Porter gets 'em all going with the first yawn.
14. C. Leave her alone, I said.
15. J. [*shouting*]. All right, dear. Go back to sleep. It was only me talking. You know? Talking? Remember? I'm sorry.
16. C. Stop yelling. I'm trying to read.
17. J. Why do you bother? You can't understand a word of it.
18. C. Uh huh.
19. J. You're too ignorant.
20. C. Yes, and uneducated. Now shut up, will you?
21. J. Why don't you get my wife to explain it to you? She's educated. [*To her*] That's right, isn't it?
22. C. [*kicking out at him from behind his paper*]. Leave her alone, I said.
23. J. Do that again, you Welsh ruffian, and I'll pull your ears off. [*He bangs Cliff's paper out of his hands*]
24. C. [*leaning forward*]. Listen—I'm trying to better myself. Let me get on with it, you big, horrible man. Give it me. [*Puts his hand out for paper*]
25. A. Oh, give it to him, Jimmy, for heaven's sake! I can't think!
26. C. Yes, come on, give me the paper. She can't think.
27. J. Can't think! [*Throws the paper back at him*] She hasn't had a thought for years! Have you?
28. A. No.
29. J. [*Picks up a weekly*]. I'm getting hungry.

Let us first look at sequencing: how the dialogue introduces, develops, and changes topics, how the speakers share their contributions. The main point is that it is Jimmy who controls what is spoken about, and, to a large extent, how Cliff and Alison join in the conversation. For their parts, Cliff and Alison— engaged in reading and in ironing—attempt to avoid involvement, to say as little as possible and so to give Jimmy the least opportunity to turn what they say against them. This strategy of reticence is not very successful, for Jimmy is very adept at turning their least words to suit his purposes. Through this conversation Jimmy asserts a series of judgements and prejudices which begin to build an impression of a 'character'.

Jimmy's opening question is rhetorical: there is no sensible answer to it. Notice the unspecific 'do this': to understand this remark (i.e. 'read the Sunday papers') we have to be aware of what in fact Jimmy is doing, and so he is assumed to be the focus of attention. He hints at the tedium of Sundays ('every', 'same'), and introduces the subject of book reviews which are indistinguishable from week to week and then (3) pretentious and obscure. The shift which Jimmy makes in 3 and 5 is characteristic. The contrastive stress on *you* implies that Jimmy himself is made to feel ignorant by the reviews, and so he might continue talking about his reactions to them; instead, he turns the word 'ignorant' into an insult to Cliff, expanded as 'peasant' in the metaphorical sense of a person who lacks knowledge and experience. Jimmy persists with this abuse in 17 and 19; Cliff concedes that he is 'uneducated' (20), a deficiency he seeks to remedy by reading the papers (24). In the interests of peace and quiet, he accepts Jimmy's judgement, but just as a plain fact about his education. Jimmy, however, nags away with the insult: 'Welsh' (23) = 'provincial' = 'peasant'.

Going back to 5, Jimmy uses the word 'peasant' a second time to initiate an attack on Alison: 'You're not a peasant are you? Here he uses the word in a more literal sense: Alison is not asked to confirm that she is not ignorant, but, literally, that she is not a member of the peasant classes. It may not be clear yet, but this is a taunt: Jimmy holds Alison's upper-middle-class background against her, and ceaselessly reviles her and her parents in these terms (11, 'White Woman's Burden', 21 'educated', etc.). The allegation Jimmy is starting here is that Alison is mindless despite and/or because of her middle-class advantages: it is implicit in 11 —the women of colonial administrators such as Alison's father have no opinions—and an explicit insult in 25-7 where Jimmy twists the meaning of Alison's and Cliff's 'think': 'She hasn't had a thought for years.' The effectiveness of Jimmy's strategy illustrates the economy of conversation between people who can make ready inferences. The one word 'peasant' allows him to launch dual, but different, assaults on Cliff and Alison. He sustains and develops his tirade by two devices. There is the technique of leaping on someone else's words and twisting them; and the starting of a verbal hare of his own, pursuing it relentlessly, and appropriating others' remarks as he goes along. The groundwork is laid for a critique of intelligence and opinions in the opening sequence about the Sunday papers. Jimmy turns this critique on to Alison by an intricate sequence of helter-skelter transitions:

7. not so brilliant after all  (i.e. despite your education and upbringing.)

10. busy
11. talk . . . talk . . . express an opinion . . . impossible to think
12. I wasn't listening properly
13. you weren't listening . . . talks . . . sleep . . . yawn  (Breaking the maxim of Relation, Jimmy implicates, through a dead metaphor, that Alison is inattentive and bored.)

15. sleep . . . only me talking
16. trying to read
17. can't understand
19. ignorant
20. uneducated  (Jimmy digresses from Alison to resume the 'ignorant' attack on Cliff; but takes care to maintain reference to Alison:)

21. Why don't you get my wife to explain it to you? She's educated.
24. trying to better myself
25. I can't think!  (A major tactical error by Alison, allowing Jimmy to climax his condemnation of her.)

26. She can't think
27. Can't think! She hasn't had a thought for years! Have you?

Alison's answer is characteristic of the way she avoids confrontation with her aggressive husband: 'No.' Subjected to this battery, her safest course is to be compliant, and brief; to give Jimmy the least possible excuse for further abuse. On this occasion he is not interested, but immediately takes up the right he has assigned himself to be the one of the three who introduces new topics, and to be utterly self-centred: 'I'm getting hungry.'

Jimmy uses another important dialogue technique, akin to implicature, to broaden the scope of his attack on Alison. This is the implying of what Labov and Fanshel call 'general propositions': beliefs or moral principles which underpin discourse and constitute ideology, but are only hinted at on the surface of the language. A system of ideas about marriage is implied from 13 on: Jimmy appeals to the general proposition that wives should be supportive of, and more specifically attentive to, their husbands. Alison unwittingly sets Jimmy going on this theme in 12 when she says 'I'm sorry. I wasn't listening properly.' Even if she means simply 'I was only half listening', the linking of the apology 'sorry' with the moral adverb 'properly' suggests that Alison acknowledges an obligation to listen attentively to Jimmy. He seizes on this implication and reinforces it in 13 and 15 with the accusation that she is bored by his talking, and, as his wife, should not be. This latter implication comes from the names he chooses to refer to himself and her, emphasizing the marital relationship—'Old Porter/Mrs Porter' in 13, the belittling husbandly endearment 'dear' in 15, and 'my wife' in 21 when he has changed the subject but evidently still has this preoccupation on his mind. His tone through this sequence is brutally sarcastic, as if he believes he has grounds for accusing her of failing in her obligations while he is fulfilling his by talking. The interest of this sequence, apart from illustrating the technique of implied propositions, is that it reveals a contradiction in Jimmy's ideology: he is berating her for breaking a convention of the bourgeois institution of marriage, an institution which he himself continually condemns and reviles. Or is he doing something more complex, mocking her for subscribing to this system and for allowing herself to be condemned by someone who does not uphold it?

I would like to comment on one more dimension of this dialogue: Jimmy's use of questions to maintain his control of the conversation.[6] Because it is so one-sided, of course, this is less of a conversation than a discontinuous tirade. Jimmy gives vent to a series of general assertions, judgements, and insults. His questions—which are never genuine requests for information or even action—serve the purpose of demanding attention while restricting the contribution of the others.

Three main types of question structure are available in English:

1. *Wh-questions*, introduced by a word such as *why*, *where*, *when*, *how*, *which*. Such questions request new information. Not surprisingly, Jimmy uses few of these, since they would have the undesired effect of admitting Cliff and Alison into the conversation, to offer their opinions and explanations. When Jimmy does use wh-questions, they are either unanswerable (1 'Why do I do this every Sunday?') or quickly followed up by another comment (17 'Why do you bother? You can't understand a word of it.') Jimmy uses wh-questions not to open up the conversation to other people's participation, but to frustrate interchange by posing vacuous questions which he assigns himself sole right to answer.

2. *Yes/No questions*, such as 'Have you finished that one yet?', request either the answer 'yes' or the answer 'no', and allow the person questioned little other freedom of reply. They are very much a feature of interrogatory discourse—for example, job interviews, doctor-patient consultations—where the interviewer is of higher status than the interviewee. Because they so severely restrict the response of the person questioned, they are felt to be impolite, and would be used sparingly in domestic conversation. Jimmy's yes/no questions are not only abrupt as such, they are also highly unfair because they contain a complexity of implication difficult to cope with in a one-word answer: e.g. 3 'Do the Sunday papers make *you* feel ignorant?' in which the complications of the stressed *you* have already been noted, or 7 'I said do the papers make you feel you're not so brilliant after all?'. The difficulties of coping with this utterance by a simple 'yes' or 'no' are formidable: 'I said' suggests that the question is in some way a paraphrase of 5 'You're not a peasant

are you?' while 'after all' implies that though Alison assumed she was educated because she was middle class (not a peasant), the Sunday papers show that she is uneducated (a 'peasant' in the sense in which Jimmy applied the word to Cliff). It is very difficult for Alison to work out what criticisms of herself she might be agreeing with or denying by whatever answer she might give, so she responds only to the most superficial meaning of the utterance: 'you have asked me a question about these papers' (wilfully misinterpreting 'the') 'which I cannot answer because I have not read them yet.'

3. *Tag questions.* These are a peculiar form with a declarative sentence as the basis and a copy of the auxiliary verb and the subject tagged on to the end, with the 'polarity' of the verb changed: if the main sentence is positive, the tag is negative, and vice versa. Jimmy uses this form several times: 5 'You're not a peasant are you?', 11, 21, 27 (with pronoun change). Tags can be very demanding, pointedly requesting confirmation of an assertion made in the main part of the sentence. They could be regarded as part of the characterization of Jimmy as aggressively demanding assent, seeking to subject his wife and his friend to his system of values. But a quite different account of the function of tags has been offered by Robin Lakoff.[7] She claims they they are a characteristic of women's speech, and that they indicate the reverse of aggression, in fact lack of confidence and a need for male confirmation of timidly held opinions. These are opposite characterizations, but they might both be relevant to Jimmy's utterances: his tags might be intended to denote aggression, but additionally connote lack of confidence. Is the bravado real? Might not the insecurity alleged of women's tags underlie Jimmy's tagging of his absurd and insulting statements? Osborne's opening stage-direction invites us to look for contradictions in the Jimmy his text has created. Further dialogic analysis of the kind begun here would, I believe, reveal how the language constructs and foregrounds these contradictions.

*Look Back in Anger* is a 'realistic' play: a fictional text in which conversational conventions evoke an illusion of recognizable people interacting through language. The language is deliberately constructed to make the dialogue seem like an overheard conversation. The assumption of realistic depiction of talk is the starting-point for the reader's or audience's engagement with the play. But this is not to say that the language is neutral, a mere representation of how people speak. The dialogue is loaded with evaluation and interpretation, the product of foregrounded structure drawing the reader or playgoer to recognition of the significant areas of the text's meaning: I have tried to show that Jimmy's ways of controlling other people, and the implied propositions to which he appeals, delineate a character of offensively aggressive behaviour but with a vulnerably contradictory system of values. How this presentation through dialogue meshes with the play's overall commentary on British 1950s society is a matter for further exploration. But the starting-point, as I have shown, could easily be an analysis of the peculiarities of dialogue which at first sight looks little out of the ordinary.

A very different dialogic technique is found in another classic play of the same vintage, Samuel Beckett's *Waiting for Godot* (1955). In this enigmatic work, two tramps, Vladimir and Estragon, wait in a barren landscape to meet a certain 'Godot'—who does not materialize, and who is, as far as one can gather, a stranger to Vladimir and Estragon anyway (if he exists). Their wait is futile, their lives are absurd and pointless, they have nothing to do or to talk about. But they talk throughout the play, interrupted only by the two incursions of Lucky and Pozzo, and the two brief visits of the Boy. Their conversation is vacuous, and often at cross purposes; in these respects it enacts the futility and meaninglessness of their existence, and by implication of human life in general.

Our apparatus for conversational analysis should, then, show failures of communication in the areas of structure where, in the other text, meaning was communicated with clarity and detail. In *Waiting for Godot*—as in many other of Beckett's works, such as *Endgame*—misfiring speech acts, misunderstanding, and incoherence are rife. In particular, Estragon doggedly misunderstands, or pretends to. To 'pass the time', Vladimir tries to tell about the thieves who were crucified with Christ:

VLADIMIR: Two thieves, crucified at the same time as our Saviour. One—
ESTRAGON: Our what?

Estragon's 'what?' instead of 'who?' claims a radical incomprehension: it refuses to acknowledge that the phrase 'our
Saviour' refers to a known human being.

> v. Our Saviour. Two thieves. One is supposed to have been saved and
> the other . . . [*he searches for the contrary of saved*] . . . damned.
> e. Saved from what?
> v. Hell.
> e. I'm going.
> [*He does not move.*]

'Saved from what?' continues a questioning which fixes on single
words and queries the application of their literal meanings. In
effect, the pointed contrast which Vladimir makes with 'damned'
forces the interpretation 'saved from hell', so Estragon's ignoring this implies his rejection of the terminology and the ideology
of the Christian myth: cf. earlier: Vladimir: 'Suppose we
repented'; Estragon: 'Repented what?' Estragon follows
Vladimir's reply with the threat 'I'm going' which in its lack of
fulfilment—*He does not move*—is typical of a whole class of
failed speech acts of both characters: a pledge to do something,
followed by a failure to do anything.

Vladimir attempts to continue his story, now concentrating on
the fact that 'of the four Evangelists only one speaks of a thief
being saved':

> v. One out of four. Of the other three two don't mention any thieves at
> all and the third says that both of them abused him.
> e. Who?

Vladimir's highly compressed account presents real difficulties
of understanding, particularly for someone who—as Estragon
protests he is—is ignorant of the story. Out of eight noun phrases
in Vladimir's two sentences, seven are based on numerals or
pronouns, words whose referents can only be identified by looking back to previous noun phrases. Since Vladimir's story has
been proceeding for some time in a scrambled fashion, with off-
putting interruptions, this elliptical speech is bound to cause
problems of cohesion (see Chapter 5). Estragon's response is so
condensed that it gives Vladimir difficulty: 'Who?' could be
asking the identity of the person(s) referred to by any of the seven
unspecific noun phrases. Common sense might suggest that the
last word, 'him', is most likely to be the queried noun phrase (the

third Evangelist or someone else?) but clearly the speaker, who knows what he means, cannot recognize the difficulty:

V. What?
E. What's this all about? Abused who?
V. The Saviour.
E. Why?
V. Because he wouldn't save them.
E. From hell?

For a person behaving as literal-mindedly as Estragon is, 'from hell' would be the correct supposition, in view of Vladimir's explanation of 'saved' earlier; but:

V. Imbecile! From death.
E. I thought you said hell.
V. From death, from death.

Estragon now raises difficulties which stress the pointlessness of the story and of Vladimir's interest in it: 'Well what of it? . . . And why not? . . . Well? They don't agree, and that's all there is to it.' Under pressure, Vladimir becomes even more terse and difficult to follow: 'But one of the four says one of the two was saved.' The story peters out, and the two tramps move apart in disgust. The importance of the story, and of Vladimir's concern with its authenticity, is undermined by the incoherence of the telling and the feigned incomprehension of the listener. The structure of the dialogue destroys the relevance of the content of the story: a central episode in Christian mythology fails to relieve the tramps' wait for Godot.

Whereas plays traditionally consist wholly of dialogue, other literary forms such as novels and short stories mix dialogue with monologic narrative and commentary. At first glance there might appear to be a very sharp distinction between passages of dialogue, where the characters' voices seem to take the stage, and passages of prose writing where the narrator takes charge. But in fact, narrative discourse engages in another class of dialogic interactions: between the narrator and the characters, and between the narrator and the reader. By 'dialogic' here I do not refer to text which has the superficial structure of dialogue, i.e. language which is set out as different 'speeches' attributed to different 'speakers'; rather, this is an implicit dialogue, where the language implies an interaction of views or values, or more overtly (see Fielding below) the presence of an attentive and thinking 'narratee'. There are a number of techniques by which the narrat*ing* voice's engagement with these narrat*ed* voices can be signified.

To begin with a very simple case, the words and phrases used to introduce speech inevitably indicate the narrator's comments on and interpretations of the utterances of the characters. Some novelists offer in this way a complete and explicit commentary on the motives and reactions of their characters; in Lawrence, for example, a 'third voice' is very obviously woven into the dialogue between two characters. For example, in Chapter 7 of *Sons and Lovers*, in addition to the routine 'he said', 'she replied' and the like, we find numerous speech-introducing expressions such as the following:

said Miriam, in her musical, caressing voice: said Miriam over-gently; laughed the farmer; she cried; replied the mother apologetically; asked Edgar, rather hesitatingly; he exclaimed appreciatively; she pleaded; he called; she laughed in fear; he remonstrated; he said suddenly; she exclaimed; he persisted; she pondered; she sang; said the child, uneasy; she murmured deep in her throat; repeated the child; she murmured; she cried; she answered, low and intense; she said hesitatingly; she said, soft and musical; he insisted; she faltered; etc.

These comments are more than 'stage-directions' giving indications of the behaviour of the speakers; cumulatively, they add an emotional colouring deriving from the narrator's analysis of the relationship between the characters. They make manifest an aspect of the narrator's ideology, in this case the positive valuation of sexual behaviour which is soft and unconfident in the woman, demanding and hyper-sensitive in the man. It is more complicated than that, but a long analysis would be necessary to refine that crude generalization. Of particular interest is the way Lawrence directly juxtaposes narrative comment with characters' statements. Readers may care to examine the chapter in question for the compatibility or otherwise of the characters' statements and the narrator's comments.

The narrator's commentary on a character and his views can also be indicated less directly, by stylistic infiltrations into the character's speech itself. A straightforward example would be stylistic parody, rendering a character's speech absurd and perhaps passing more specific comment; for instance Dickens's treatment of the union demagogue Slackbridge in *Hard Times*:

'Oh my friends, the down-trodden operatives of Coketown! Oh my friends and fellow-countrymen, the slaves of an iron-handed and a grinding despotism! Oh my friends and fellow-sufferers, and fellow-workmen, and fellow-men! I tell you that the hour is come, when we must rally round one another as One united power, and crumble into dust the oppressors that too long have battened upon the plunder of our families, upon the sweat of our brows, upon the labour of our hands, upon the strength of our sinews, upon the God-created glorious rights of Humanity, and upon the holy and eternal privileges of Brotherhood!'

This is obviously a caricature of oratory, but its specific features are significant: repetition, parallelism, alliteration, excessive and trite adjectives, worn-out and melodramatic metaphors, add up to a hyperbolic language which is alien from his artisan audience and distant from workaday reality. Much more could be shown by a detailed analysis, but my intention here is merely to illustrate how a character can be criticized within the very language he is made to utter.

There are other formats for implicit dialogue between author and character; but no space to give a survey here. For one very subtle instance of another kind of dialogic structure, see the delicate interweaving of narrator's and character's voices in a free indirect discourse passage from Joyce's story 'Eveline', discussed in Chapter 9, pp. 139–40 below.[8]

There is one important type of implicit dialogue in which the writer creates a narrating voice juxtaposing authorial views with those ascribed to his presumed *readers* or *narratees*, in addition to whatever dialogue with the characters is going on. This was very prominently a feature of eighteenth- and early nineteenth-century narrative discourse. Laurence Sterne, who used the technique extensively and exuberantly, also described it aptly:

Writing, when properly managed, (as you may be sure I think mine is) is but a different name for conversation: As no one, who knows what he is about in good company, would venture to talk all;—so no author, who understands the just boundaries of decorum and good breeding, would presume to think all: The truest respect which you can pay to the reader's understanding, is to halve this matter amicably, and leave him something to imagine, in his turn, as well as yourself.

(*Tristram Shandy*, 1759–67)

'Conversation' with the reader is found throughout Fielding's *Tom Jones* (1749) from which I take my final example for this chapter: the first introduction of Miss Bridget Allworthy, Squire Allworthy's sister. Here is the paragraph in full:

1. He now lived, for the most part, retired in the country, with one sister, for whom he had a very tender affection. 2. This lady was now somewhat past the age of 30, an aera, at which, in the opinion of the malicious, the title of old maid may, with no impropriety, be assumed. 3. She was of that species of women, whom you rather commend for good qualities than beauty, and who are generally called by their own sex, very good sort of women—as good a sort of woman, madam, as you would wish to know. 4. Indeed she was so far from regretting want of beauty, that she never mention'd that perfection (if it can be called one) without contempt; and would often thank God she was not as handsome as Miss such a one, whom perhaps beauty had led into errors, which she might have otherwise avoided. 5. Miss Bridget Allworthy (for that was the name of this lady) very rightly conceived the charms of person in a woman to be no better than snares for herself, as well as for others, and yet so discreet was she in her conduct, that her prudence was as much on the guard, as if she had had all the snares to apprehend which were ever laid for her whole sex. 6. Indeed, I have observed (tho' it may seem unaccountable to the reader) that this guard of prudence, like the trained bands, is always readiest to go on duty where there is least danger. 7. It often basely and cowardly deserts those paragons for whom the men are all wishing, sighing, dying, and spreading every net in their power; and constantly attends at the heels of that higher order of women, for whom the other sex have a more distant and awful respect, and whom (from despair, I suppose, of success) they never venture to attack.

Fielding here expresses, indirectly, a complex ironic judgement on Miss Allworthy. The complexity of statement and tone derives from the implicit presence of voices and opinions other than Fielding's: I want to show, briefly, how the language creates an impression of dialogue within a literally monologic text. I shall then demonstrate how the reader (who is centrally implicated in this 'dialogue') is called upon to interpret the text through a process which is constantly at work in understanding conversations: reference to general propositions or stereotypes which encode different views on social issues, in this case on sexual morality.

Fielding's standard mode of discourse is a kind of pretend-dialogue with an implied reader. This fiction is constructed by foregrounding first- and second-person expressions ('I', 'you' and related forms) and other address and reference items relating to the addressee who is invoked ('the reader', 'madam'); by verbs emphasizing the narrator's speech acts (not prominent in this particular paragraph, but I am thinking of verbs like 'acquaint', 'digress', 'desire', 'plead' in the next); by modal expressions of judgement as to values and judgement as to narrative knowledge ('with no impropriety', 'perhaps', 'very rightly', 'unaccountable', 'I suppose'). The frequent presence of these devices in the text creates an impression of a vociferous and opinionated narrator, speaking his views and demanding response from a reader whom he appears to confront face-to-face. Readers should feel bombarded with assertions, and badgered to take up views of their own.[9] Often, Fielding's attitude to a subject is clearly announced, and whatever agreement or disagreement he expects from his reader is equally clear. But as often again, the attitudes involved are complex, and ironically expressed: and that is the situation in this paragraph.

The general drift of the critique is clear: Miss Bridget is attacked for an ostentatious, hypocritical and self-deluding self-righteousness; for an envious and malicious contempt of beauty, and an unnecessary and excessive defence of her own virtue. But Fielding never *says* this; in fact, in some ways he appears to say quite the reverse—seems to approve of aspects of Miss Bridget's behaviour which he actually condemns. What he does is set up Miss Bridget as an instance of a category—'She was of that species of women'—and then insinuate his own views by citing other people's responses to that category (including Miss Bridget's). In this way he passes the burden of judgement from himself on to society. The sets of people cited are as follows:

a. 'that higher order of women' of whom Miss Bridget is an instance
b. 'their own sex'
c. 'the men . . . the other sex'
d. 'the malicious'

The voices and attitudes of these groups come through in various degrees of directness. Differences of style within the passage are instructive. Whereas the last two sentences, 6–7, are elaborately metaphorical, a literary signal of the narrator's presence, by contrast other sentences and phrases verge on the colloquial. In 3, 'called . . . very good sort of women—as good a sort of woman, madam, as you would wish to know' seems not only to report the opinion of the category 'their own sex' but their voice also: this could be felt to be a virtual quotation of one woman (from category b) speaking, probably sarcastically, about type a. The next sentence, 4, quotes Miss Bridget—very damagingly, since what she is reported as saying habitually is extremely petty and slanderous, immediately undermining 'good' in the previous sentence so that it has to be read ironically. These quasi-quotations enhance the dramatic effect or verisimilitude of the dialogic style, but more importantly they complicate the rhetorical relationship between narrator and reader. Fielding is able to damn Miss Bridget not through his own words but through the statements of others, including herself, while he, having established an ironic rhetoric, is even able to appear to approve attitudes which he in fact condemns: see 5 'Miss Bridget Allworthy . . . very rightly conceived . . .'. The reader has no voice quoted, but is faced with the task of locating, in this maze, Fielding's view.

We make sense of this passage by interpreting what is said (which is not what is meant) in terms of a series of implicit general propositions conveying sexual stereotypes. The generalizing phrase 'that species of women' in sentence 3 gives notice that such a stereotype is to follow. What characteristic properties does society attribute to this species? The relative clause does not really define their attributes without further interpretation, because it is doubly ambiguous: first, we need to be told what these 'good qualities' are; Fielding's vagueness here is crucial, because he can then proceed to bring us gradually to a realization that these good qualities are in fact vicious qualities. Second, 'rather than' in 'you rather commend for good qualities than beauty' does not clearly specify the nature of the option presupposed. Do we commend such women for their good qualities, ignoring their beauty because it is irrelevant? or do we commend them for good qualities because they have no beauty for us to commend? In sentence 4, the phrase 'want ["lack"] of beauty'

directs us to the second, unsympathetic, meaning, while not effa-
cing the suggestion of innocent commendation first given by sentence 3. The proposition that supplies the ideological basis of the
whole passage (even if it is strongly attacked) is, A, that sexual
abstinence is commendable in women. There is a related stereotype, B, that beautiful women are sexually active (and are so
outside the bounds of society's moral code) and therefore, by A,
are to be condemned. A more worldly proposition, C, alleges that
men are only interested in beautiful women. Now C is obviously
basic to sentences 6 and 7, but let us stay with the context of the
opening of the paragraph for a moment. Acknowledging the
possible validity of C—even if one dislikes its cynicism—casts
unfavourable light on the motives of women who profess A: thus
we derive the stereotype D, that plain women profess virtue
because, being plain, they lack sexual opportunity. The pro-
testation of virtue is not a good quality in itself (even if one
applauds the idealism of A over the worldliness of C) because its
motive is suspect: it is likely to be a type of compensatory behaviour. Interpretation in these terms helps with the slightly puzzling
word 'assumed' in sentence 2: 'old maid' is not just a gibe at the
sexual isolation of these ladies (in which case the title might have
been 'given', not 'assumed'); it is a taunt at the willing assumption of the *role* of old maid. The behaviour associated with this
role, and specifically Miss Bridget's behaviour, is sketched in the
following sentences: it may be summarized as vicious slander
masquerading as righteous comment; and ostentatious (and of
course pointless) sexual aloofness ('prudence').

Fielding locates Miss Bridget Allworthy within a nest of
ideological contradictions in the area of sexual behaviour and
'moral' behaviour. This ironic and ambivalent siting is functional in setting up her future role in the plot. But over and above
this narrative relevance is the fundamental implication of the
narrator and the reader in these ideological dilemmas which are
essentially dilemmas provoked by discourse rather than by story.
As we have seen, the text of this passage does not say what it
means, but can only be interpreted in the light of some unstated
propositions, commonplaces of the culture, which the reader
must supply. It is incriminating to entertain these stereotypes,
which are variously naïve, malicious, cynical, but readers must
put themselves in the position of formulating the hidden proposi-

tions in order to make any sense of the passage. This gives Fielding the opportunity to cast his readers as people who might hold the propositions as convictions rather than just imagine them as hypotheses. In sentence 3, Fielding directly invokes a class of female readers presumed to approve of proposition A (the virtues of celibacy) and then leads them on towards B in sentence 4 by suggesting, in the parenthesis '(if it can be called [a perfection])', that he agrees with this censorious attitude towards beautiful women; an illusion sustained in sentence 5 'very rightly'. The parenthetical comments in 6 and 7 convey a mock naïveté, feigned innocence of the worldly proposition C and the cynical conclusion D. But the metaphorical and hyperbolic language of these last two sentences, with the parody of romantic sentiment ('all wishing . . .') makes it clear that Fielding is being ironic at the expense of any gullible and self-righteous reader. The emergence of the frankly critical proposition D revaluates what has gone before, and reinterprets the attitudes of sentences 3–4 as hypocrisy and unkindness; and damns any reader who has gone along with the surface meanings of the early part of the paragraph. Fielding's dialogue with the reader encourages the latter to approve of Miss Bridget, and to think that Fielding does, but subverts this position in the very process of expounding it.

## Notes

1. See M. Coulthard, *An Introduction to Discourse Analysis* (London: Longman, 1977).
2. See J. L. Austin, *How to Do Things with Words* (London: Oxford University Press, 1962); J. R. Searle, *Speech Acts* (London: Cambridge University Press, 1969); P. Cole and J. L. Morgan, eds., *Speech Acts* (New York: Humanities Press, 1975).
3. See his 'Logic and Conversation', reprinted in the Cole and Morgan volume cited in note 2 above.
4. See G. N. Leech and M. H. Short, *Style in Fiction* (London: Longman, 1981) Ch. 9.
5. W. Labov and D. Fanshel, *Therapeutic Discourse* (New York: Academic Press, 1977).
6. See Ch. 4, 'Interviews', in R. Fowler, R. Hodge, G. Kress and A. Trew, *Language and Control* (London: Routledge and Kegan Paul, 1979).
7. Robin Lakoff, *Language and Woman's Place* (New York: Harper and Row, 1975).

8. For further examples see my *Linguistics and the Novel* (London: Methuen, 1977). Ch. 4.
9. Because the terms of debate for the issues Fielding raises have changed so much, modern readers are likely to be in a more detached position; but an imaginative reconstruction of the arguments Fielding mounts is likely to be that much more defamiliarizing.

# 9

# Point of View

In traditional discussions of novels, short stories, epic, and other forms of narrative writing, it is usual to draw a distinction between the story and the point of view from which the story is narrated. For instance, the events of George Eliot's *Middlemarch* or *The Mill on the Floss* would be said to be narrated from the point of view of an 'omniscient' narrator who has privileged access to the thoughts and feelings of the characters in a way that an ordinary external observer does not; and who can foresee how events are going to turn out in the future. By contrast, the narrators in Hemingway's novels and stories say little about the characters' feelings. A third type of point of view is represented in Virginia Woolf's novels: the events of the narrative are viewed from the perspective of one or more of the characters, with great emphasis on the characters' private responses to people and events. These three examples are merely illustrations from some familiar authors, and they by no means complete the range of types of point of view. In this chapter I have room to analyse only some of the more striking variations in point of view, with particular attention to defamiliarized perspectives; some other relevant materials are discussed in the following chapter.

Three senses of the phrase 'point of view' may be usefully distinguished: *psychological* point of view; *ideological* point of view; and *spatio-temporal* point of view.[1] The easiest to understand is the last. *Temporal* point of view refers to the impression which a reader gains of events moving rapidly or slowly, in a continuous chain or isolated segments; it includes also disruptions of the 'natural' flow of time, by for example flashbacks, previsions or the interweaving of stories which concern different time-spheres. The *spatial* dimension of spatio-temporal perspective corresponds to viewing position in the visual arts. Just as a painting is composed structurally so that the viewer seems to see some objects close up, some in the distance, some focused, and some less clear; so that the eye moves from one part of the painting to another in an apparently natural succession—in the same way, someone who reads a novel which represents objects, people, buildings, landscapes, etc., is led by the organization of the language to imagine them as existing in certain spatial relationships to one another and to the viewing position which he feels himself to occupy. In the following highly pictorial passage setting the opening scene of a novel, we can see very easily what parts of language contribute to the building of spatial point of view:

The last of a hanger ran under the eastern ridge of the combe, where it had always been too steep and stony for the plough. It was now little more than a long spinney, mainly of beech. The field sloped from the wall of trees, westward, a gentle bosom, down to the open gate on to Fishacre Lane. The dark coats lay there in against the hedge, covering the cider-jar and the dinner-bundle, beside the two scythes that had been used to clear the still-dewed hedge swathe much earlier that morning. Now the wheat was half cut. Lewis sat perched behind the faded carmine reaper, craning into the sea of blond stems for stones, his hand on the mower-lever, always ready to lift the blades. Captain hardly needed the reins; so many years of plodding, just so, down the new stubble next to the still-standing ears. Only at the corners did Lewis cry, softly, coaxing the old horse round. Sally, the younger horse, who had helped on the steeper ground, stood tethered beneath a thorn not far from the gate, cropping the hedge, her tail intermittently swishing.

Bindweed ran up the stems of the corn; seeding thistles, red poppies; and lower, the little cornfield violets called heart's-ease; with blue speedwell eyes and scarlet pimpernel, shepherd's glass, herb of the second sight. The field's name was the Old Batch—batch from bake, some ancient farm's own annual bread was always grown there. The sky's proleptic name was California; the imperial static blue of August.

There are four figures in the field, besides Lewis on the reaper-binder.

(John Fowles, *Daniel Martin*, 1977, pp. 7–8)

This descriptive passage continues for another two pages, gradually introducing four men, a boy, and two horses harvesting within the field, and a momentary onlooker outside it. If you read the whole passage, you will notice a wave-like alternation of visual perspectives, starting with an illusion of 'long shot', moving to 'close-up' as each of the people is introduced in turn, with distant views placed between the individual portraits. The opening four sentences give the broad outlines of the field: a ridge with a narrow belt of trees to the east, the field itself a more gradual slope to the west, bounded by a hedge with a gate in it. The general view is given by naming the features of landscape themselves ('ridge', 'combe', etc.) and also by the metaphorical use of other terms with strong and clear geometrical connotations ('wall', 'bosom', 'sea', and 'corners' later), with a few quantitative adjectives ('long', 'steep', 'steeper'). The components of this landscape are held together by prepositional phrases indicating relationships and directions: 'under the ridge', 'from the wall', 'down to the open gate on to Fishacre Lane', etc. Such locative phrases are exceptionally frequent throughout this and similar descriptive passages, and they have a double function: first, by sheer frequency, in co-operation with other types of locative ('where', 'westward', 'there', etc.) they insist on the spatial content of the prose, they foreground the theme of the representation of a place and its component parts. But the prepositions and adverbs of place do not simply *refer* to locations, they also *relate* them, and as the text is organized in sequence, the reader scanning it left-to-right is led from place to place in a definite order, with a starting-point and a subsequent development which suggest an initial viewing position and a chain of perceptions moving from that position. Here the reader's eye is led from a vantage-point high in the field, along the 'wall of trees', then down towards the hedge with the coats, food, and tools stowed near it. The sequence offered by the relational prepositions of place is helped by some unobtrusive deictic verbs which indicate movement in a certain direction, or a certain positioning: 'ran under', 'sloped from . . . down', 'covering'. Notice how 'covering', a very ordinary word, implies vision from above: the observer sees the coats on top of the food. When the observer's eye has reached the hedge, it is moved, by implication, back into the centre of the field ('the wheat was half cut') to focus on Lewis on the reaper. At this point the emphasis is largely on his physical attitude— 'perched' etc.—but the verb 'craning' shifts to his perspective: he looks down into the corn for stones, and what he sees, which is not what the distant observer could see, is detailed in the microscopic next paragraph: 'Bindweed . . . seeding thistles . . . and lower, the little cornfield violets . . .' There is a striking difference of scale here, but soon the perspective moves out again to the wide view: 'There are four figures . . .' and in the following paragraph, 'They work in two teams, on opposite sides of the field, one clockwise, the other anti-clockwise, stooking' which is clearly the panoramic viewpoint of the high, distant observer.

The whole passage is worth studying for the mechanics of these visual movements and transitions. The author's control of the reader's perception—focus, survey, and scanning of relationships—is strict, and dependent on linguistic artifices which though unobstrusive are clearly defamiliarizing since the language instructs us to perceive carefully, clearly, slowly, and relevantly.

(Another rich source of techniques of spatial perspective is the novel *Titus Groan* by Mervyn Peake—who was also a painter—from which illustrations are taken for other purposes later in this chapter.)

More fundamental than spatial point of view, and rather complicated because they overlap, are the *ideological* and *psychological* planes of point of view. I will introduce *ideology* first, briefly, reserving various parts of my treatment to the relevant categories of psychological point of view and to Chapter 10. The basic sense of 'ideology' has already been given in Chapter 2. I do not mean the derogatory sense of the word ('false consciousness' or 'delusion') but simply the system of beliefs, values, and categories by reference to which a person or a society comprehends the world. As we have seen, language performs a crucial role in stabilizing, reproducing, and changing ideology. Now when we speak of point of view on the plane of ideology in a narrative text, we mean the set of values, or belief system, communicated by the language of the text. A novel, for example, gives an interpretation of the world it represents, a fact which is central to the interpretative descriptions offered by literary critics. The content of the ideology—Tolstoy's Christianity, Lawrence's celebration of sexuality, Orwell's denunciation of totalitarianism, and so on—is one thing to be identified, and in the next chapter I shall show how effective linguistic analysis is in demonstrating the presence of such themes and ideas.

Other questions arise in considering point of view on the ideological plane. First, who, within the compositional structure of the work, is the vehicle for the ideology? Is it the author speaking through the narrative voice, or is it a character or characters? And is there a single dominating world-view, or a plurality of ideological positions? The least interesting cases are those in which the text projects a single normative set of values according to which all the scenes, events, and characters are judged: such cases are rare, and among the major novels potential candidates turn out to be complex or ironical—the perpetually commenting author–figure 'Fielding' in *Tom Jones*, the central consciousness Strether in Henry James's *The Ambassadors*. Plural ideological structure is more interesting, and particularly when the different value-systems articulated in the work are in some conflicting relationship. In Dickens's *Hard Times*, for instance, various groups of characters represent and voice a number of different social theories: Gradgrind and Bounderby the values of utilitarianism and manufacturing capitalism; Stephen Blackpool and Rachael loyalty and affection; the circus people, spontaneity and gaiety; and so on. These points of view, which are expressed in many distinct and contrasting linguistic styles, are constantly challenging and contradicting each other, giving the novel an argumentative, dynamic structure. There is not one overall world-view subordinating every philosophy to a single point of view, but a range of alternative and interacting views of life.

Point of view on the ideological plane may be manifested in two fairly distinct ways, one direct and one less so. Both ways of establishing ideological perspective are clearly identifiable in specific areas of linguistic structure.

In the first case, a narrator or a character may directly indicate his or her judgements and beliefs, by the use of a variety of *modal* structures. Modality (cf. p. 57 above) is the grammar of explicit comment, the means by which people express their degree of commitment to the truth of the propositions they utter, and their views on the desirability or otherwise of the states of affairs referred to. Respectively, 'Sir Arthur *certainly* lost his fortune at the gaming table' and 'His gambling was *disastrous* for the family'. I have italicized the modal words: they come from a fairly specialized section of the vocabulary, and are easy to spot. The forms of modal expression include:

*modal auxiliaries*: may, might, must, will, shall, should, needs to, ought to, and a few others. These words signal caution or confidence, to various degrees: something might happen, something will happen, must happen. Notice that the strongly positive modals such as 'must' have the additional meaning of necessity or even obligation, so that a speaker using such a word to indicate his judgement of certainty or truth may simultaneously express approval of or a demand for the things that are being spoken of.

*modal adverbs or sentence adverbs*: certainly, probably, surely, perhaps, etc. There are also adjectival versions in such constructions as 'It is certain that . . .'.

*evaluative adjectives and adverbs*: lucky, luckily, fortunate, regrettably, and many others.

*verbs of knowledge, prediction, evaluation*: seem, believe, guess, foresee, approve, dislike, etc.

*generic sentences*: these are generalized propositions claiming universal truth and usually cast in a syntax reminiscent of proverbs or scientific laws: 'For loan oft loses both itself and friend, /And borrowing dulls the edge of husbandry' (Polonius); 'At sixteen, the mind that has the strongest affinity for fact cannot escape illusion and self-flattery . . .' (George Eliot, *The Mill on the Floss*). Often generics are blatantly ironic, as the opening sentence of *Pride and Prejudice* quoted above (p. 57). Where irony is not intended, the writer may vary her syntax somewhat away from the proverbial form, rendering the generic less obtrusive. George Eliot often does this: for instance, from the same chapter of *The Mill on the Floss*, 'It was a dark, chill, misty morning, likely to end in rain—one of those mornings when even happy people take refuge in their hopes'. From sentences like this, the reader cumulatively builds up a picture of the stock of 'common sense' (i.e. ideology) on which George Eliot depends in presenting and evaluating the world of her characters.

(For a further instance of the relationship between modality and ideological structure, see the passage from Fielding's *Tom Jones* in the discussion of the author's dialogue with the reader, pp. 121–5 above.)

There is a perhaps even more interesting sense in which language indicates ideology or, in fiction, the world-views of author or characters. The modal devices just discussed make explicit (though sometimes ironic) *announcements* of beliefs; other parts of language, indirectly but nevertheless convincingly, may be *symptomatic* of world-view: it has traditionally been assumed in stylistics that the different ways people express their thoughts indicate, consciously or unconsciously, their personalities and attitudes. A writer may create a narrator, or a character, whose language expresses a characteristic or idiosyncratic point of view; and the style may be adjusted as the book progresses to express ideological development. Linguistic criticism, under the influence of M. A. K. Halliday's model of analysis, has developed sophisticated techniques for describing implicit ideology. This is such an important topic that I have reserved substantial discussion of it until the next chapter, on language and world-view. I can, however, refer to two very familiar examples. In *A Portrait of the Artist as a Young Man*, Joyce changes the style gradually to reflect the intellectual development of Stephen Dedalus as he grows from infant to undergraduate, from the limited consciousness of the baby through the perplexity and isolation of the schoolboy, the fantasizing and emotionally self-indulgent adolescent, to the dogmatic, alienated college student. To focus a little more closely on a text, consider the famous opening sentences of Faulkner's *The Sound and the Fury*:

Through the fence, between the curling flower spaces, I could see them hitting. They were coming toward where the flag was and I went along the fence. Luster was hunting in the grass by the flower tree. They took the flag out, and they were hitting. Then they put the flag back and they went to the table, and he hit and the other hit. Then they went on, and I went along the fence. Luster came away from the flower tree and we went along the fence and they stopped and we stopped and I looked through the fence while Luster was hunting in the grass.

(William Faulkner, *The Sound and the Fury*, 1931)

The character from whose point of view this part of the narrative is told is Benjy, a 33 year-old man with the mind of a young child. It is obvious that Faulkner has designed the language to suggest the limitations of Benjy's grasp of the world around him. The style is not, however, disintegrated in a haphazard fashion, but systematically patterned in certain areas of structure. Most striking is a consistent oddity in *transitivity*: there are almost no transitive verbs with objects, a preponderance of intransitives ('coming', 'went', 'hunting', etc.) and one transitive ('hit') used repeatedly without an object, ungrammatically. It is implied that Benjy has little sense of actions and their effects on objects: a limited notion of causation. Second, Benjy uses *circumlocutions* to designate objects that he has no name for: 'the curling flower spaces', 'where the flag was', 'the flower tree'. The implication of this is that he has command of only a part of his society's classi-fication of objects. Third, he uses *personal pronouns* in an odd way—'them . . . they . . . They . . . they . . . they . . . he . . . the other . . .'—without identifying who he is referring to and with-out varying the words he uses to refer to them. Fourth, his *deictic* words—'Through . . . between . . . coming toward where . . . went along,' etc.—do not add up to a comprehensible picture of the positions and movements of the golfers, himself, and Luster: Benjy is literally disoriented, with little sense of his location and his relationships within a context. The four areas of structure which characterize Benjy's world-view—transitivity, lexical classification, reference, and deixis—recur in other linguistic constructions of ideology, as we shall see in the next chapter.

We come now to the third major sense of 'point of view', that which Uspensky calls *'psychological'* or (better) *'perceptual'* point of view. This concerns the question of who is presented as the observer of the events of a narrative, whether the author or a participating character; and the various kinds of discourse asso-ciated with different relationships between author and character. For clarity's sake, I have divided the field into two categories each with two subtypes; but I must stress that probably no text exemplifies any single type purely and consistently: such con-sistency would be an inconceivable technical *tour de force* in a medium as complicated as language. In any case, a great deal of the interest, in fictional narrative texts, is in the shifts, contrasts, and tensions between various modes of observation within the text, as we shall see in the extract from Mervyn Peake's *Titus Groan* analysed at the end of this chapter.

The basic distinction is between *internal* and *external* perspec-tive. Uspensky introduces the distinction, without its further complexities, thus:

When an author constructs his narration, he usually has two options open to him: he may structure the events and characters of the narrative through the deliberately subjective viewpoint of some particular indivi-dual's (or individuals') consciousness, or he may describe the events as objectively as possible. In other words, he may use the *données* of the perceptions of one consciousness or several, or he may use the facts as they are known to him. (p. 81.)

'Internal' narration is, then, narration from a point of view within a character's consciousness, manifesting his or her feelings about and evaluations of the events and characters of the story (which I shall call type A); or from the point of view of someone who is not a participating character but who has knowledge of the feelings of the characters—the so-called 'omniscient' author (type B). 'External' point of view relates the events, and describes the characters, from a position outside of any of the protagonists' consciousnesses, with no privileged access to their private feelings and opinions (type C), and in some cases actually stressing the limitations of authorial knowledge, the inaccessibility of the characters' ideologies (type D).

The most subjective form of internal perspective, type A, consists of first-person narration by a participating character, or third-person narration strongly coloured with personal markers of the character's world-view or including internal monologue. The first-person variant is distinguished *deictically* by prominent use of first-person singular pronouns and perhaps some use of present tense, referring to the 'present time' of the act of narration (rather than referring consistently to the past time of the narrated events). The presence of a participating narrator may be highlighted by foregrounded *modality* stressing his judgements and opinions. There is reference to the character–narrator's feelings and thoughts by the use of *verba sentiendi* (see below)—a very obvious subjectivity. Choices of *diction* may individualize the narrator as a certain psychological type or a member of a certain social class (cf. *lexical register* below). Finally, syntactic patterns, *transitivity*, etc. may endow the character with a certain ideological position (cf. the discussion of Benjy above, and Chapter 10 below). Most of these linguistic characteristics are ·found in Nick Carraway's introduction of himself in the opening pages of *The Great Gatsby*:

In my younger and more vulnerable years my father gave me some advice that I've been turning over in my mind ever since.

'Whenever you feel like criticizing any one,' he told me, 'just remember that all the people in this world haven't had the advantages that you've had.'

He didn't say any more, but we've always been unusually communicative in a reserved way, and I understood that he meant a great deal more than that. In consequence, I'm inclined to reserve all judgements, a habit that has opened up many curious natures to me and also made me the victim of not a few veteran bores. The abnormal mind is quick to detect and attach itself to this quality when it appears in a normal person, and so it came about that in college I was unjustly accused of being a politician, because I was privy to the secret griefs of wild, unknown men. Most of the confidences were unsought—frequently I have feigned sleep, preoccupation, or a hostile levity when I realized by some unmistakable sign that an intimate revelation was quivering on the horizon; for the intimate revelations of young men, or at least the terms in which they express them, are usually plagiaristic and marred by obvious suppressions. Reserving judgements is a matter of infinite hope. I am still a little afraid of missing something if I forget that, as my father snobbishly suggested, and I snobbishly repeat, a sense of the fundamental decencies is parcelled out unequally at birth.

(F. Scott Fitzgerald, *The Great Gatsby*, 1925)

Some form of the 'I' pronoun occurs in every sentence but one, often several times. Modality is very prominent in two areas: evaluative adjectives and adverbs, and generic sentences. Evaluative modalizers include 'more vulnerable', 'unusually', 'curious', 'veteran bores', 'abnormal', 'normal', 'unjustly', etc. Generics are extremely frequent: 'all the people . . .', 'The abnormal mind . . .', 'for the intimate revelations . . .', 'Reserving judgements . . .', 'a sense of the fundamental decencies . . .' Ironically, Nick believes that he is 'inclined to reserve all judgements', but constantly makes pronouncements on life and on people in the most pompous way imaginable. His vocabulary—slightly staid, formal and moralistic—fits this ironized self-characterization very aptly; the effect is cumulative, rather than locally salient, and derives from phrases such as 'unusually communicative', 'privy', 'feigned', 'intimate revelation', 'plagiaristic', 'fundamental decencies'. Also appropriate to Nick's view of the world is the rather literary, measured syntax. One is struck, for instance, by double adjective phrases such as 'younger and more vulnerable', and numerous balanced parallel phrases: 'curious natures . . . veteran bores', 'the abnormal mind . . . a normal person', 'as my father snobbishly suggested, and I snobbishly repeat'. The generics, too, are in a blatantly proverbial syntax. Finally, Nick's language includes many *verba sentiendi*, as Uspensky calls them: words denoting feelings, thoughts, and perceptions, primary signals of a subjective point of view. Nick, being preoccupied with himself and his image, refers often to his own inner processes: 'turning over in my mind', 'understood', 'inclined', 'victim', 'realized', 'afraid'. Notice that a lot of these are words denoting reflection and judgement. In the ironic context which Fitzgerald has created, we are bound to suspect the objectivity of someone who is so self-conscious, so confident and considered in his pronouncements.

Benjy's language illustrates a different kind of first-person subjective perspective. As we saw, the emphasis there was less on explicit modality and personal judgement than on the construction of a radically transformed syntax and semantics imitating peculiar patterns of thought and perception. This shaping of language towards an illusion of directly experienced mental process is the central technique in the familiar type of internal point of view known as *stream of consciousness* or *internal monologue*. The Joycean variety associated with Bloom in *Ulysses* provides the best-known examples; within third-person narration, there are sudden shifts into first-person discourse in which Bloom seems to speak his loosely associated, incomplete thoughts:

He walked on. Where is my hat, by the way? Must have put it back on the peg. Or hanging up on the floor. Funny, I don't remember that. Hallstand too full. Four umbrellas, her raincloak. Picking up the letters. Drago's shopbell ringing. Queer I was just thinking that moment. Brown brilliantined hair over his collar. Just had a wash and brushup. Wonder have I time for a bath this morning. Tara Street. Chap in the paybox there got away James Stephens they say. O'Brien.

Deep voice that fellow Dlugacz has. Agenda what is it? Now, my miss. Enthusiast.

(James Joyce, *Ulysses*, 1922)

The second type of internal perspective, B, differs from type A in being consistently third-person narration by an 'omniscient' author who claims knowledge of what is going on in the characters' heads, reporting their motives and feelings. Deixis and modality are basically the property of the author–narrator, who can thus locate himself in an ideological and spatio-temporal position independent of the characters. But authorial modality is not prominent (contrast external type D below) since the focus is on the characters, not on the position from which they are described.

To a greater or lesser degree, the author gives an account of the mental processes, feelings, and perceptions of the characters, so the chief linguistic marker of this variant of internal narration is the presence of *verba sentiendi* detailing intentions, emotions, and thoughts. In the following extract from Mervyn Peake's *Titus Groan* (1946), the kitchen boy Steerpike, who is about to escape from captivity by scaling a wall, examines and plans his route; it is a moment of concentrated thought and intense response, and so there is a high density of *verba sentiendi* (italicized):

Again he *fastened his gaze* upon the first dozen feet of vertical stone, *choosing* and *scrutinizing* the grips that he *would use*. His *survey* left him *uneasy*. It *would be unpleasant*. The more he *searched* the wall *with his intense eyes* the less he *liked* the *prospect*, but he could *see* that it was feasible if he *concentrated* every *thought* and fibre upon the attempt.

In internal perspective type B, transitivity patterns and systems of lexical classification may or may not indicate the world-view of a character; to the extent that they do, they are framed by the authorial ideology. In the example just quoted, the verbs 'choosing' and 'scrutinizing' analyse rather than dramatize Steerpike's thoughts: they are the author's words for internal processes, part of an extensive lexical system by which Steerpike is characterized throughout the book as a deliberate, calculating entrepreneur. The point is that the words themselves are not manifestly part of any personal discourse attributed to Steerpike with a claim of psychological mimesis as we would expect in internal narration of type A.

The difference between type A (internal and wholly subjective) and type B (internal but allowing an authorial phrasing of the character's feelings) provides the basis for an important style which throws types A and B into what, in the last chapter, I called an implicitly dialogic relationship. This style is *free indirect discourse* (FID): internal perspective in which the character's subjective feelings, given in type A narration transformed into third person, are interwoven with and framed by the author's account of the character's inner state (type B).[2] By this device an author is able to juxtapose two sets of values, to imply a critique of the character's views without the direct judgement which an external perspective would produce. Some particularly sensitive intermingling of the two internal viewpoints is found in Joyce's *Dubliners* stories (1914), from which I quote the opening of 'Eveline'. Eveline is a shop-girl who has agreed to elope to Buenos Aires with her boy-friend Frank; on the eve of her departure she weighs up the pros and cons of this adventure as against the ties of her admittedly hard family life, looking after her violent father and two younger children after her mother died insane. She cannot leave her mundane and unhappy family life, and does not depart with Frank. Like most of the Dubliners in this collection of stories, she is spiritually paralysed, bound to her trivial life by inaction and apathy. Her static and passive posture at the beginning of the story is symbolic of her inner state:

She sat at the window watching the evening invade the avenue. Her head was leaned against the window curtains, and in her nostrils was the odour of dusty cretonne. She was tired.

Few people passed. The man out of the last house passed on his way home; she heard his footsteps clacking along the concrete pavement and afterwards crunching on the cinder path before the new red houses. One time there used to be a field there in which they used to play every evening with other people's children. Then a man from Belfast bought the field and built houses in it—not like their little brown houses, but bright brick houses with shining roofs. The children of the avenue used to play together in that field—the Devines, the Waters, the Dunns, little Keogh the cripple, she and her brothers and sisters. Ernest, however, never played: he was too grown up. Her father used often to hunt them in out of the field with his blackthorn stick; but usually little Keogh used to keep nix and call out when he saw her father coming. Still they seemed to have been rather happy then. Her father was not so bad then; and besides, her mother was alive. That was a long time ago; she and her brothers and sisters were all grown up; her mother was dead. Tizzie Dunn was dead, too, and the Waters had gone back to England. Everything changes. Now she was going to go away like the others, to leave her home.

The first paragraph is third-person narration with some internal perspective—'she was tired'—but nothing that would indicate Eveline's own consciousness; indeed, quite the reverse, with the very literary metaphor of the evening 'invading the avenue'. Later, we find the phrasing of the opening paragraph repeated with slight variation after two and a half pages: 'The evening deepened in the avenue . . . she continued to sit by the window, leaning her head against the window curtain, inhaling the odour

of dusty cretonne.' This repetition is another indication of the
author's presence, but only in retrospect, so the first paragraph
on first reading is more neutral than writerly. But as paragraph
two progresses, the language develops in the direction of a style
definitely associated with Eveline. From 'One time . . .', all the
sentences can be transformed into utterances which might be
spoken by Eveline simply by changing some third-person pronouns into first—'in which we used to play'—and some past
tenses into present—'Tizzie Dunn is dead'. At the end of the
paragraph the tense is in part explicitly present: 'Everything
changes. Now she was . . .' 'Now' is repeated frequently in the
story. It is the present tense of the character's reflecting consciousness, framed by the past tense of the author's narration.
This mixture of two deictic spheres is very characteristic of FID.

Other signs of the character's voice are a general colloquialism
tending towards the childish when she remembers her childhood
experience: this is obvious both in the vocabulary and in the
opaque use of pronouns as if their referents were understood.
The subjective and non-literary tone is given also by an exclama-
tion immediately after our extract—'Home!'—and continues
throughout the story: 'What would they say of her in the Stores
when they found out that she had run away with a fellow? Say she
was a fool, perhaps.' Eveline's voice is recognizable throughout
the story, but the indirect third-person report (as opposed to the
direct report of stream of consciousness) prevents her point of
view from becoming alienated from that of the author, main-
taining sympathy. Every now and then, Joyce intervenes not with
a judgement but with a formulation of the shop-girl's dilemma
which is patently not phrased in the language that the story has
established as hers: 'Besides, the invariable squabble for money
on Saturday nights had begun to weary her unspeakably', 'that
life of commonplace sacrifices closing in final craziness'. The
authorial voice reminds us that there are alternative ways of
thinking about her situation; that, although Eveline 'tried to
weigh each side of the question', the terms which she possesses
for this self-examination are inadequate to the task: she cannot
break out from her own limited ideology. The double voice of
FID allows Joyce to present and to question her attitudes virtually simultaneously; to place two sets of values in an implicit
dialogue with one another.

Turning now to external perspective, its basic characteristic is avoidance of any account of the thoughts or feelings of characters, or at least avoidance of any claim to the fidelity of such an account. As with the internal modes, there are two chief variants. What I refer to as type C is the most impersonal form of third-person narration, impersonal in two respects. First, in relation to the characters, it declines to report their inner processes, and so *verba sentiendi* are as much as possible banished from the discourse; it claims to be objective in not offering to report what an ordinary unprivileged observer could not see. Second, it is impersonal in relation to the author or narrator, declining to offer judgements on the characters' actions; this claimed authorial objectivity is indicated by avoidance of evaluative modalities. Type C is the formula for the most neutral, impersonal, type of third-person narration, which we associate with epic among the older literatures and, in the modern period, with the ideal of objective realism proposed by Flaubert; and with news reporting. Hemingway is thought to be an extreme practitioner of this kind of writing, but close examination of his work reveals that the impression of objectivity comes from a foregrounding of action verbs and descriptions of physical states, with a relative scarcity but not a complete absence of modals and of words of feeling. In some of the more 'deadpan' parts of his work, we find passages such as the following which are almost entirely sequences of action predicates and physical descriptions, with speech directly reported without comment:

Outside the arc-light shone through the bare branches of a tree. Nick walked up the street beside the car-tracks and turned at the next arc-light down a side-street. Three houses up the street was Hirsch's rooming-house. Nick walked up the two steps and pushed the bell. A woman came to the door.
'Is Ole Andreson here?'
'Do you want to see him?'
'Yes, if he's in.'
Nick followed the woman up a flight of stairs and back to the end of a corridor. She knocked on the door.
'Who is it?'
'It's somebody to see you, Mr Andreson,' the woman said.
'It's Nick Adams.'
'Come in.'
Nick opened the door and went into the room. Ole Andreson was lying

on the bed with all his clothes on. He had been a heavyweight prize-
fighter and he was too long for the bed. He lay with his head on two
pillows. He did not look at Nick.

(Ernest Hemingway, 'The Killers', 1928)

This is unusually close to pure type C external, but the story as a
whole does contain a few phrases indicating internal states, and a
few modal judgements. It is virtually impossible to remove all
modal and psychological indicators from a text, but they can, as
above, be kept at a minimal level of prominence.

Finally we come to type D external perspective. By contrast
with the impersonal type C, the persona of the narrator is high-
lighted, perhaps by first-person pronouns and certainly by
explicit modality. By these means, the impression is created of a
speaker who controls the telling of the story and who has definite
views on the world at large (announced in generic sentences,
perhaps) and on the actions and characters in the story (evaluative adjectives). Externality in relation to the characters emerges
when the narrator's modal activity includes what Uspensky calls
*words of estrangement*: words such as 'apparently', 'evidently',
'perhaps', 'as if', 'it seemed', etc. as well as metaphors and
comparisons. These expressions pretend that the author—or
often, one character observing another—does not have access to
the feelings or thoughts of the characters. They emphasize an act
of interpretation, an attempt to reconstruct the psychology of the
character by reference to the signs that can be gleaned by external
observation. *Verba sentiendi* may be used, but only if introduced
by words denoting appearance or speculation: 'He seemed tired,'
'She was probably furious.' There is also, in texts which make
extensive use of this technique, considerable reference to the
physical characteristics and gestures of the characters. All of the
linguistic signs of external type D narration are copiously present
in the following extract, from the opening of a novel; I have italicized the 'words of estrangement':

On an autumn afternoon of 1919 a hatless man with a slight limp *might
have been observed* ascending the gentle, broad acclivity of Riceyman
Steps, which lead from King's Cross Road up to Riceyman Square, in the
great metropolitan industrial district of Clerkenwell. He was rather less
than stout and rather more than slim. His thin hair had begun to turn
from black to grey, but his complexion was still fairly good, and the rich,
very red lips, under a small greyish moustache and over a short, pointed

beard, were quite remarkable in their *suggestion* of vitality. The brown eyes *seemed* a little small; they peered at near objects. As to his age, an experienced and cautious observer of mankind, without previous knowledge of this man, *would have said* no more than he *must* be past forty. The man himself was *certainly* entitled to say that he was in the prime of life. He wore a neat dark-grey suit, which *must have been* carefully folded at nights, a low, white, starched collar, and a 'made' black tie that completely hid the shirt-front; the shirt-cuffs could not be seen. He was shod in old, black leather slippers, well polished. He gave an *appearance* of quiet, intelligent, refined and kindly prosperity; and in his little eyes shone the varying *lights* of emotional sensitiveness.

(Arnold Bennett, *Riceyman Steps*, 1923)

This is very straightforward: the physique and dress are detailed, and the deductions from them which a stranger would make are suggested. A more extreme form of external type D point of view uses the words of estrangement, usually accompanied by metaphors, to alienate the character, setting him at a distance, without sympathy. Grotesques and villains are often presented in this way. It is not only that the emphasis on their physical peculiarities presents them as bizarre and threatening; the exaggerated refusal to go *below* the surface, the ostentatious guesses at what unimaginable motives might lurk beneath, present the characters as inhuman, beyond the comprehension of an ordinary human belief system. Examples of this alienating use of external type D point of view are quoted in the discussion of switching perspectives in *Titus Groan* which follows.

Mervyn Peake's *Titus Groan* (1946) is a long, complicated novel, gothic and sinister but also comic in an almost Dickensian fashion: there is a large cast of grotesque characters all marked by strong idiosyncrasies including, prominently, peculiarities of physique, dress, and movement. The individual characters are presented as isolated within their own private worlds of motive and sensation; they are single-minded in the manner of 'humours'; Swelter is animated by his plotting of revenge on Flay, the Countess totally preoccupied with her birds and cats, Sourdust lives for the ritual of the community and its administration, Steerpike is ambitious to dominate the castle and its inhabitants for his own personal interest.

The mixture of isolation and detailed motivation is managed compositionally by constant and abrupt switches of perspective.

The text focuses with precise concentration on one character at a
time, but this focus is moved systematically from character to
character. When a character is acting alone, s/he is often given
exclusive attention; when a group is assembled, individuals are
picked out one by one for their gestures and responses to one
event, then the story develops and Peake goes the rounds again.
Both internal perspective (type B, omniscient) and external perspective (type D, estranged) are employed, with frequent sharp
changes from one to the other. Internal type B conveys knowledge of people's motives and reactions, whereas external type D
presents them as aliens, as caricatures. The source of type B is, by
definition, the framing narrative discourse; type D sometimes
emanates from the narrator's point of view, sometimes that of
one character watching another. There seems to be almost no
trace of internal type A ('mimetic'), so that, when we watch one
person with another's eyes, the defamiliarizing metaphors used
are as flamboyant and 'literary' as those of the narrator, and do
not communicate a character's world-view distinct from that of
the narrative voice.

I want to refer briefly to a crucial scene of the novel for some
contrasting techniques: switches of perspective from internal to
external; within internal perspective, switches from character
to character; the defamiliarizing use of external perspective in
the transformation of human to grotesque or to machine; and
accompanying alternations of spatial point of view. The scene is
a violent encounter between Swelter, the cook, and Flay, Lord
Sepulchrave's personal servant, just before the christening of
Titus, the infant heir to the Gormenghast estate. I cannot quote
the whole section, pp. 102–5 in the Penguin edition, and must
assume that it will be read carefully in its entirety. For ease of
reference, I have numbered the relevant paragraphs as follows:

1. Great activity . . . . 2. Suddenly the door opened . . . 3. 'Woah . . .' 4.
The door knob moved . . . 5. Flay stiffened . . . 6. Swelter, as soon . . .
7. A voice came out of the face . . . 8. The line of . . . 9. Although Mr
Flay . . . 10. Swelter, as Mr Flay spat . . . 11. Into the room . . . 12. 'Mr
Flay . . .' 13. This was brought out . . .

Spatial: para 1 establishes the setting—'the cool room'—and an
observation point—'in the room'. The room is empty but from
within the room an invisible observer, a viewing point occupied

by the narrator and the reader, watches Flay enter; note the deictic 'came' indicating movement towards the viewer: 2 'Suddenly the door opened and Flay came in.' Flay's external appearance and his movements around the room are described and then he is located at the point of observation: 2 'he heard a voice beyond the door.' Para 4 presents the emergence of Swelter in the door opening, from the psychological and visual viewpoint of Flay: 4 'For some time, or so it seemed to Flay, taut areas of cloth evolved in a great arc and then at last above them a head around the panels and the eyes embedded in that head concentrated their gaze upon Mr Flay.' Through this estranged, metaphorical language we feel that Flay sees Swelter as a shape, not as a person; but the visual viewpoint switches from Flay to Swelter at the end of the sentence. From now on we see Flay from Swelter's point of view, and vice versa, in alternating perspectives. Both see one another as objects, and so does the reader see both. Estranged external D narration is the dominant mode, presenting both characters as grotesque automata. However, some internal perspective is reserved for Flay, and some clauses of active transitivity.

Paras 2, 5, and 8 contain some phrases externalizing and estranging Flay: 2 'The negative dignity of the room threw him out in relief as a positive scarecrow', 2 'he shot his chin forward like a piece of machinery'; 5 'Flay stiffened—if it is possible for something already as stiff as a piece of teak to stiffen still further'; 8 'The line of Mr Flay's mouth, always thin and hard, became even thinner as though scored with a needle.'

The estranged external treatment of Flay is modest, however, compared with the externalization of Swelter. I have referred to para 4, which presents him as a massive configuration of 'areas of cloth'. There are also classic markers of estranged external— diverse grotesque metaphors, modalizers such as 'as though', 'seem', evaluative adjectives—attached to Swelter in paras 6, 7 ('a voice came out of the face'), 8 ('the white mountain'), 9, 10, and 13. Para 6 illustrates the technique at its peak of intensity:

Swelter, as soon as he saw who it was, stopped dead, and across his face little billows of flesh ran swiftly here and there until, as though they had determined to adhere to the same impulse, they swept up into both oceans of soft cheek, leaving between them a vacuum, a gaping segment like a slice cut from a melon. It was horrible. It was as though nature had lost control. As though the smile, as a concept, as a manifestation of pleasure, had been a mistake, for here on the face of Swelter the idea had been abused.

Swelter receives virtually no internal treatment. The only *verba sentiendi* attributed to him in the whole passage are 'saw' (para 6) and 'gazed' (10). Where an internal alternative would have been possible, an external expression is preferred: Swelter does not 'concentrate' on Flay, but wears 'an expression of comic concentration' (10). Flay's responses and perceptions, however, are frequently mentioned: for example, 2 'cared', 'to his mind', 'defiance', etc.; 9 'learned', 'ignore', 'his pride was wounded', 'learned', 'hatred'. For this reason we are 'on Flay's side' in his feud with Swelter: it is not only that Swelter is the more hideous of these two ogres—though that certainly is the effect of the estrangement devices piled on the cook—but also that Flay's feelings, through the reserving for him of internal type B treatment, remain accessible to us. He could hardly be called sympathetic, but his actions are motivated and comprehensible:

as he suddenly strode past the chef towards the door . . . he pulled the chain over his head and slashed the heavy brass links across the face of his taunter. (para. 13)

This narrative climax is signalled by the appropriate transitivity structure of action clauses, as happens at other crucial points in the narrative, for instance the moments of greatest effort and decisiveness in Steerpike's escape over the castle rooftops. Technically this is external narration type C ('Hemingwayan'), but in the context it involves the reader with Flay by presenting him as determined and active.

## Notes

1. I adapt the classification offered by Boris Uspensky, trans. Valentina Zavarin and Susan Wittig, *A Poetics of Composition* (Berkeley: University of California Press, 1973).
2. See Brian McHale, 'Free Indirect Discourse: A Survey of Recent Accounts', *Poetics and the Theory of Literature*, 3 (1978), 249–87.

# 10
# Meaning and World-View

In Chapter 2, I argued that language is of great importance in shaping speakers' classification of experience: as Halliday puts it, language has an *experiential* or *ideational* function. Applying this notion to a whole language, one could claim that English as a whole, or French, or Arabic, encodes two sorts of meanings which are accessible to speakers: natural meanings such as 'red', 'greater than', 'square', 'up/down' which are necessarily coded because all human beings are biologically equipped to make such discriminations; and on the other hand social meanings which reflect the organization of a society and its relationship with its environment: 'Prime Minister', 'son', 'doctor', 'democracy', 'landscape', 'Spring', etc. It is obviously in the—vast—area of social meanings that differences between languages are greatest; and, if the ideational theory is correct, speakers' world-views differ most in this socially constructed field of significances.

Just one point to emphasize here is that, when I speak of 'social meanings', I am not referring only to terms like 'aunt' or 'vote' which are obviously directly defined in terms of social organization. The point about the social construction of reality is that it extends to many concepts that we normally regard without question as natural and fundamental: 'common sense' terms like 'home', 'anger', 'food' (cf. my discussion of 'weed' and 'pet', p.. 18 above). Languages vary considerably in what meanings they encode even in what one might regard as basic areas and structures of experience.

I referred above to the ideational resources of 'the whole language'. This broad generalization allows us to say that English differs from French ideationally, an obvious fact which emerges from the well-known difficulties of translation between languages. But comparing whole languages is an unmanageable task, and anyway remote from the particularity of real language-use. At that level the ideational differences we are conscious of are differences between speaker and speaker, text and text. This is how Halliday relates his 'ideational function' to the experience of the individual:

Language serves for the expression of content: it has a representational, or, as I would prefer to call it, an *ideational* function . . . the speaker or writer embodies in language his experience of the phenomena of the real world; and this includes his experience of the internal world of his own consciousness: his reactions, cognitions, and perceptions, and also his linguistic acts of speaking and understanding.[1]

Now experience, and its coding in language, differ from individual to individual: not absolutely, nor randomly, but according to conventions which govern the individual's roles in the social and economic system. S/he is born into a family at a specific place in a much wider social network, with access to some patterns of interaction and not to many others; similarly, specific limitations of experience and contacts extend through school, work, and the social affiliations of maturity. In consequence, our experience and thus what we know about and need to have coded in our semantic resources, is personal but is also a product of our position in socio-economic relations. Under these constraints, our semantic repertoire and the structure of our language are similar to the resources of people who have had similar paths through life, and significantly different from others.

The same ideational variation distinguishes text from text: each act of language is formed for a specific purpose and in a particular setting, and the text's structure reflects these circumstances. The social setting and the purpose of the communication produce a characteristic set of meanings, these are coded in a characteristic structure of the text, and this is the relevant ideational shaping for the persons concerned. Again, differences are not random: a text's structure, and thus its perspective on its subject-matter, follows the *conventions* for that particular type of communication in that type of setting. To offer a simplified extreme example, the textual and therefore ideational structure of a love-letter is likely to be very different from that of a sociological paper on courtship, even though the subject-matter might be similar. The differences would reflect conventional contrasts of goals, social roles, assumptions about the reader, assumptions about other relevant discourse, etc. Differences of world-view would be relatable to conventionalized, socially based, perceptions of communication.

Now the same person might well write a love-letter and an academic article; and many other types of discourse. The point is that every person's socio-linguistic abilities are diverse, so that their language-use incorporates a repertoire of ideational perspectives. It would be incorrect to think that each individual possesses one single, monolithic, world-view or ideology encompassing all aspects of his or her experience; rather, the ideational function provides a repertoire of perspectives relative to the numerous modes of discourse in which a speaker participates. When I say 'X's point of view' or 'X's world-view', I am using a shorthand for 'the viewpoint constituted for X in this mode of discourse'.

This pluralism is part of the reason why, as Halliday observes, the extreme version of the Whorf hypothesis of linguistic determinism (that one is absolutely constrained, conceptually, by the structure of one's own language) cannot be correct. A language embodies way*s*, not *one* way, of looking at the world, and in these circumstances it is obvious that speakers are not going to be trapped within one overriding system of beliefs. Because speakers constantly make ideological shifts as they change modes of discourse (and are frequently involved in contradictions—which can readily be brought to consciousness) they can experience a creative relativity of view. As Halliday puts it: 'The speaker can see through and around the settings of his semantic system; but he is aware that, in doing so, he is seeing reality in a new light, like Alice in Looking-glass House' (p. 333). Obviously, knowledge of more than one language must help speakers to be aware of ideational restrictions imposed by their native linguistic competence. So must experience of a multiplicity of modes of discourse within their own language: an experience which should be a prime objective in critical education. Finally, if we recall the argument about language and defamiliarization presented in Chapter 4, it should be clear that texts in 'literary' modes of discourse are expected to help us see around the settings of our semantic systems, to be aware of new ideational orderings, 'reality in a new light'.

Ideational processes may be significant either at some specific point in a text (a *local* effect) or by a *cumulative* building of a world-view. I will be primarily examining the latter case. That is not to say that locally effective ideational processes are not important. Local processes include some of the most powerful of traditional rhetorical devices, the 'figures of thought' ranging from the complex concept-forming apparatus of metaphor[2] to surprising and challenging lexical choices, as when T. S. Eliot opens a poem with the conundrum 'polyphiloprogenitive'. Local devices may suggest specific reinterpretations of experience at particular points in the text; many examples have already been given in this book. Cumulative ideational structuring depends on regular and consistent linguistic choices which build up a continuous, pervasive, representation of the world. This is the major source of point of view in fiction. Cumulative ideational structuring is of course a property of all discourse, not just those modes which are regarded as 'literary'. We may notice a distinctive style in a speaker, a newspaper, a writer, a novel, etc. (or we may not notice it—it may register automatically and unconsciously if habitualized) and this is the product of regularly repeated choices of linguistic structure. Such regularities establish particular varieties or *registers* of discourse such as legal language, scientific writing, popular journalism, romantic fiction, etc., or more specifically the style of an author or of a school of writers. Within the context of the present argument, the point is that such stylistic or register differences, correlating with social and ideological circumstances, carry differences of ideational significance. So the distinctive linguistic style of, say, a political speech necessarily implies a particular perspective on the topics treated: that politician's view of the world as shaped for that particular occasion of discourse. Concrete examples of how different styles shape reality differently can be found in Tony Trew's analyses in *Language and Control* of news-reporting styles.[3] Different papers' treatments of the same events, he argues, reflect and express contrasting theories of the causes, nature, and significance of the events.

Discussing this phenomenon in literary fictions, I have called it *mind-style*: the world-view of an author, or a narrator, or a character, constituted by the ideational structure of the text.[4] From now on I shall prefer this term to the cumbersome 'point of view on the ideological plane' which I borrowed from Uspensky in the previous chapter: the notions are equivalent. The basis for the idea, and much of the linguistic analysis required to make it concrete, are provided by M. A. K. Halliday in a pioneering article 'Linguistic Function and Literary Style: An Inquiry into the Language of William Golding's *The Inheritors*'[5]. Here Halliday demonstrates how foregrounded patterns of *transitivity*—what processes, participants and circumstances feature in clauses—are used by Golding to suggest cognitive limitation, a diminished sense of causation and an imperfect understanding of how humans can control the world, on the part of the central character, Lok, a Neanderthal man whose world is being taken over by a more advanced people. Halliday's article is absolutely essential reading for this part of linguistic criticism.

I shall illustrate ideational structuring involving three different types of linguistic feature: *vocabulary, transitivity*, and certain *syntactic structures*.

As we have seen, the *vocabulary* speakers command is a strong influence on, and indicator of, the range and structuring of their experience. The ideational and thematic importance of vocabulary in texts has long been recognized by literary critics, so I am not going to treat it at length; the contribution of linguistics to the study of vocabulary is to ground it in the semantic and psychological theory sketched in the early chapters, and to suggest a system of terms for lexical analysis.

Once we look at vocabulary or *lexis* as the encoding of ideas or experience, it becomes a good deal more dynamic than a dull list of words in a dictionary. The lexical structure of a text, or of a person, can be thought of as a distinctive, but changing, set of relations and processes.

The basic process, the background against which the others work, is *lexicalization*. This is simply the existence of a word for a concept—'magnolia' for magnolia—and of sets of words for families of concepts—'bush', 'shrub', 'tree'. Normal lexicalization has been adequately discussed in Chapter 2: the theory that the lexis of a person, or of a discourse, or of a society, can be regarded as mapping the conceptual repertoire of the person (etc.) concerned. If we do not know the term 'magnolia', we are likely not to know the concept which it denotes; if we designate the woody part of the plant kingdom with a different set of terms from 'bush', 'shrub' and 'tree', it is likely that we classify that part of our experience differently. Before moving on to variations on the normal situation, I want to make one further point:

that different terms are available for referring to the same object. They may differ, first, in connotation because their origins are in different registers: 'house' versus 'domicile' or 'knackered' versus 'tired'. Stylistic differences stemming from differences of connotation are well understood in literary studies and need no further comment here. The second dimension of variation is less familiar in stylistics, and that is variation in generality or abstractness of terms. 'Shrub' is a more general term than 'magnolia', and conversely 'apple' is a more specific word than 'fruit', 'fruit' more specific than 'thing', and so on. It would be possible for a writer consistently to choose general terms, or specific terms, in a text, with consequent differences of effect. This is a possibility which I have not investigated thoroughly in textual analysis, but it seems likely that consistent over-generalization would create the impression of mind-styles tending to childishness, naïveté, coyness, evasiveness. One example that comes to hand is Mr Tulliver's repeated use of 'thing' in his shy and unfluent consultation with Mr Riley about his son's education: 'There's a thing I've got in my head . . . It's a very particular thing . . .' and so on; see George Eliot, *The Mill on the Floss* (1860), Bk. I, Ch. 3. On the other hand, consistent use of very specific terms would evoke specialist knowledge, pedantry, obsession, etc.; examples should not be hard to find. Such effects would be akin to those of *underlexicalization* and *overlexicalization*, my next topics.

*Underlexicalization* is lack of a term or of a set of terms. The psycho-linguistic theory of vocabulary that we have been assuming would suggest that such gaps, in an individual's lexical repertoire, mean that the individual does not have access to the concepts concerned, or has difficulty of access. In deliberately formed 'literary' texts such as we have been considering, underlexicalization is marked by two alternative linguistic devices: either the noticeable suppression of a term, or the substitution of a noticeably complex expression for what in other registers would be a simple term. The former procedure, suppression, is the basis of Swift's shocking presentation of the Yahoos as animals rather than humans (p. 43 above). The latter, substitution of a complex expression, is a standard device for the evocation of naïve consciousness, as we have seen already in Benjy's 'curling flower spaces' and 'flower tree'. (Note that lexical suppression is also at work in the opening of *The Sound and the Fury*: the game of golf which Benjy is watching is never named.) Lok in the text discussed by Halliday is assigned phrases like 'white bone things', 'a lump of bone', 'sticky brown stuff'. In Kingsley Amis's *Take a Girl Like You* (1960), the inexperienced heroine Jenny Bunn, taken to a pretentious restaurant, contemplates the 'huge pink fish', 'raw fish' (smoked salmon?), 'sort of meat fritter' (paté?), 'curly iron fences' (wrought iron) incomprehendingly.

In such cases, the concept or object which is presumably unfamiliar to the perceiving subject is rendered by a circumlocution, a noticeably complex phrase where we would have access to a simpler term securely coding the concept.[6] The complexity of the circumlocution foregrounds the device, signals the reader to be alert for implied significance. Now the circumlocution conveys, not just lack of a securely coded concept, but an *analysis* in the cognitive area where the gap lies. In this respect, circumlocutions with their different internal structures can function very differently. Benjy's 'flower tree' and Jenny's 'raw fish' are simple cases: the naming is done by an accurately applied noun of higher generality preceded by a mundane descriptive modifier. Neither of these phrases specifies the nature of the entity referred to to any extent, leaving the concept vague and unprocessed. Benjy's 'curling flower spaces', on the other hand, does not simplify, but attempts to analyse a complicated geometrical concept: 'Through the fence, between the curling flower spaces, I could see them hitting.' Read in context, the noun phrase 'curling flower spaces' seems not to be a laborious struggle to a concept for which there might be a simple word which Benjy does not know, but the creation of a perception which Benjy has and which is unusual (a strangely shaped space edged by the shapes of the flowers), thus defamiliarizing, for 'normal' speakers of English. This creative effect shows that underlexicalization, avoidance of the simple and most efficient term, is by no means always a case of a cumbersome second best.

For a clearly poetic use of this 'analysing' type of circumlocution, consider lines 4–6 of Wallace Stevens's poem 'Disillusionment of Ten O'Clock' (1915):

> The houses are haunted
> By white night-gowns.
> None are green,

Or purple with green rings,
Or green with yellow rings,                    5
Or yellow with blue rings.
None of them are strange,
With socks of lace
And beaded ceintures.
People are not going                           10
To dream of baboons and periwinkles.
Only, here and there, an old sailor,
Drunk and asleep in his boots,
Catches tigers
In red weather.                                15

The white night-gowns, in this context, symbolize a humdrum
lack of imagination, a failure in the solid citizen to experience
'strangeness' as the drunken sailor does. The alternative imagina-
tions are symbolized by, first, a simply coded but presumably
extravagant colour, green, and then by a series of colour combinations which are not lexicalized in English: 'purple with green
rings', etc. The reader must exercise his imagination to work out
the appearance of these striking garments, and here the internal
structure of the phrases is significant: notice how the colour of
the rings in line 4 adopts the background green of line 3, while
lines 5 and 6 reverse the process by adopting the colour of the
rings as the colour of the background. The reader's attention is
carefully led back and forth between figure and ground, with
heightened consciousness. The unsettling underlexicalization is
accompanied by other defamiliarizing lexical processes with ideational implications: the double meanings of 'disillusionment'
and 'haunted', the odd syntax of 'socks of lace', the archaism
'ceintures', and so on. Although this is not an obscure poem, its
lexis is sufficiently unfamiliar to lead the reader into an estranged
perception of the world (one which the wearers of plain white
night-gowns do not share).

*Overlexicalization* is, as its name suggests, the opposite process: the availability, or the use, of a profusion of terms for an
object or concept.[7] Strictly speaking, it is the existence of many
synonyms or near-synonyms, but it is useful to generalize from
the specialized phenomenon of synonymy to include other,
similar, lexical processes. There are cases where a text makes

extensive and repetitive use of sets of terms for related concepts, so that particular lexical systems, and the ideas they symbolize, become foregrounded. Fairly straightforward literary examples abound, and have been amply discussed in literary criticism. A proliferation of terms in some semantic field indicates an unusual preoccupation with a part of the culture's, or the writer's, experience. Shakespeare, and other writers, have been virtually psychoanalysed by the critics on the basis of recurrent lexical preferences; other critical notice of cumulative vocabulary patterns has been more moderate, interpreting them as indicators of theme or point of view.

I can illustrate the specific working of overlexicalization by referring briefly to a poem which everyone knows: Keats's 'To Autumn' (1820). Here the writer draws repeatedly on a restricted lexical stock in the area of experience which is the poem's central preoccupation.

> Season of mists and mellow fruitfulness,
>     Close bosom-friend of the maturing sun;
> Conspiring with him how to load and bless
>     With fruit the vines that round the thatch-eaves run;
> To bend with apples the moss'd cottage-trees,
>     And fill all fruit with ripeness to the core;
>         To swell the gourd, and plump the hazel shells
>     With a sweet kernel; to set budding more,
> And still more, later flowers for the bees,
> Until they think warm days will never cease,
>     For Summer has o'er-brimm'd their clammy cells.

The rhetorical device here is hyperbole: celebratory, praiseful overstatement. The key word for Keats's theme of the abundance of autumn is repeated three times: 'fruitfulness', 'fruit', 'fruit'; and the fruits of autumn are particularized in 'vines', 'apples', 'gourd', 'hazel', 'flowers'—admittedly, not closely related fruits of nature, but nevertheless a dense set of similar references for a short stretch of text, and clearly forming a coherent class in Keats's mind. Among the attributes emphasized are the centres of the fruit, mentioned in two near-synonymous words, 'core' and 'kernel'; notice how the lexical relationship is underlined by phonetic parallelism in the consonants /k/ and /r/. The maturing of the fruits is extensively lexicalized, using three pairs of words which convey three processes: weighing down ('load', 'bend'), swelling ('swell', 'plump'), and filling with liquid ('fill', 'o'er-brimm'd'). As with 'kernel' and 'core', two of these are so close in meaning as to be almost synonyms—'plump', 'swell'; for another example of near-synonymy, cf. 'maturing' and 'ripeness'. The fullness of the vocabulary in these lexical fields (working with phonological and syntactic repetitiveness) draws attention to, and imitates, the natural plenitude which is Keats's theme.

We now move from *vocabulary* to a 'deeper' level of meaning. In Chapter 5 (pp. 54–5) I mentioned some basic semantic relations in terms of which the propositions conveyed by sentences are organized: concepts such as 'agent', 'object', 'action', 'mental process'. These (and others) form what Halliday calls the *transitivity* system of a language: they are a small set of presumably universal categories which characterize different kinds of event and process, different types of participants in these events, and the varying circumstances of place and time within which events occur. In the article on Golding's *The Inheritors* referred to above, Halliday has shown how consistent selections from the transitivity system can suggest different world-views, including, as in the example he discusses, highly defamiliarized mind-styles. I shall follow the broad outlines of Halliday's system, without adopting all the specific terminology of his analysis, which is somewhat idiosyncratic.

I have explained that the semantic nucleus of a proposition is a predicate and one or more nouns associated with it. Predicates convey some sort of activity or state in which the associated nouns are concerned. They divide into several contrasting types. A fundamental type is *action* proper, a movement or deliberate action with consequences, under the control of the principal noun:

1. The horse *swam* across the river.
2. John *slammed* the door.

These contrast on the one hand with *states* which simply attribute properties to objects:

3. The road is *wide*.
4. This music is too *loud*.

and contrast in another dimension with *processes* which are events or changes which 'happen' to things without their control:

5. John *fell*.
6. The road *widened*.

There are also *mental processes* and *mental states*:

7. Henrietta *listened*.
8. Brian was *blissful*.

These simple distinctions between different types of events and states of affairs convey different pictures of what is going on in the world. It is easy to imagine the types of mind-styles associated with a dominance of one sort of pattern: predominant action predicates may go with strong physical activity, foregrounded mental processes with an introspective mind-style, and so on. But to complete such an analysis we need also to make reference to the kinds of nouns which occur with predicates.

Nouns designate individual concepts and entities; and in propositions, they do not only designate or refer, but also have their referents performing different *roles* relative to predicates. There is a fundamental contrast of role between *agent* and *object*:

9. *John* jumped twenty feet.
10. *John* fell twenty feet.

In 9 John is treated as a person acting deliberately, in 10 as a mere physical object to which something outside his voluntary control happens. Both agent and object roles occur in 11:

11. The kitten chased a butterfly.

It is useful to distinguish sub-types of 'object', including *beneficiary*:

12. Mary sent *Henrietta* a Christmas card.

and *experiencer*:

8. *Brian* was blissful.
13. *Helga* is in love.
14. *We* heard an explosion.

Another role needed in this type of analysis is *instrument*:

15. I picked the lock with a *hairpin*.

Now for some complications. In 15 the word 'with' gives an indication of the role of the noun. However, while some roles are marked by prepositions, as here, and some by the position of the noun in the sentence, as in 9, and 16 below, English does not invariably identify roles, unlike Latin which, with both prepositions and case-endings, is much more informative in this respect. This lack of explicit role-marking can have ideationally interesting consequences when a noun with one role is made to appear as if it had another. For instance, the classic position for the agent role is the left-hand noun phrase in a clause:

16. *John* slammed the door.

But none of the following italicized nouns are agents; the syntax makes them *appear* to be, and cumulatively this sort of construction might suggest an analysis of depicted events as more active than might be:

17. The *door* slammed.          (Object)
18. A *hairpin* picked the lock.  (Instrument)
19. *John* loves Mary.           (Experiencer)
20. *I* received a telegram.      (Beneficiary)
21. The *gale* blew down the fence. (Force)

Such 'pseudo-agentive' structures are important in the passage from *Melmoth the Wanderer* to be analysed shortly.

Finally, to complete the account, I will mention the nouns which perform as 'circumstances'. The principle is simple: to the basic structure of a proposition can be added noun phrases which specify times and places:

22. Mary sent Henrietta a card *last Christmas*.
23. I'd like to be a fly *on the wall*.

There is a 'pseudo-locative' construction which depersonalizes people by representing them as places:

24. *In the majority of babies* there is a strong sucking instinct.

With this basic apparatus at hand, we can now examine how transitivity patterns determine mind-style. I have chosen a characteristic extract from Charles Maturin's Gothic novel *Melmoth the Wanderer* (1820) in which an estranged mind-style is constructed by peculiar transitivity.

As Melmoth leaned against the window, whose dismantled frame, and pieced and shattered panes, shook with every gust of wind, his eye encountered but that most cheerless of all prospects, a miser's garden— walls broken down, grass-grown walks whose grass was not even green, dwarfish, doddered, leafless trees, and a luxurious crop of nettles, and weeds rearing their unlovely heads where there had once been flowers, all waving and bending in capricious and unsightly forms, as the wind sighed over them. It was the verdure of the churchyard, the garden of death. He turned for relief to the room, but no relief was there—the wainscotting dark with dirt, and in so many places cracked and starting from the walls—the rusty grate, so long unconscious of a fire, that nothing but a sullen smoke could be coaxed to issue from its dingy bars,—the crazy chairs, their torn bottoms of rush drooping inwards, and the great leathern seat displaying the stuffing round its worn edges, while the nails, though they kept their places, had failed to keep the covering they once fastened,—the chimney piece, tarnished more by time than by smoke, displayed for its garniture half a pair of snuffers, a tattered almanack of 1750, a time keeper dumb from want of repair, and a rusty fowling piece without a lock . . .

The Gothic genre indulges its heroes and heroines in morbid feelings and sensational imaginings. The most straightforward way of indicating their broodings and forebodings would be a foregrounding of mental state and mental process predicates, with overlexicalization of morbid sentiment, and that is the pattern of many works in this genre. But this passage works in a linguistically more complex fashion; and this may be the reason why its style can still be experienced as alert and defamiliarizing rather than (as much Gothic) stale and formulaic. Melmoth's mental state is not described, but is to be inferred from his perception of the objects around him. His surroundings are perceived as active, sentient, like living beings, whereas he is inactive, a mere register of impressions. Melmoth is subject of only two verbs ('leaned' and 'turned') and these are simply movements which reorient his body, first to the window and then to the room. His survey of the garden seems not to be a conscious looking, but an accident of vision: 'his eye encountered', Melmoth performs no action which causes a change to any object; he does not control his environment, nor even interact with it.

By contrast, the objects in his environment engage in a welter of activity; action predicates abound: 'frame, and . . . panes, shook', 'weeds rearing their . . . heads . . . waving and bending', 'the wind sighed', 'wainscotting . . . starting from the wall'; 'the . . . seat displaying the stuffing', 'the nails . . . kept . . . failed to keep', 'the chimney piece . . . displayed . . .'. The obvious linguistic point is that there is a large number of clauses in which a noun referring to an inanimate object serves as the subject of an action predicate: the sheer quantity of these clauses is the basis for our impression of an unexpectedly vigorous objective world. The individual clauses might be quite ordinary ('panes shook') or contain dead metaphors ('the wind sighed'); but the effect is cumulatively grounded. However, there is much more going on in this passage, for many of the individual clauses are unusual. Particularly notable are the subject-verb combinations in the section describing the room: the wainscotting is not just loose but 'starts' from the wall; the seat, nails and chimney-piece are all given verbs which denote purposeful actions, implying conscious intention (e.g. 'displayed'). This is in a context which contains other indications of consciousness or feeling in objects— 'cheerless', 'capricious', 'unconscious', 'sullen', 'crazy'—or words which in some respect might be associated with humans— 'dwarfish', 'doddered', 'heads', 'dumb'. It is not surprising that the plants and furniture that occupy the garden and the room are sensed to be animate: the weeds rearing their heads like aggressive wild beasts, the 'time keeper' (with its *-er* suffix ambiguous between agent as in 'teacher' and instrument as in 'screwdriver') felt to be more like a chronicler than a clock.

Other aspects of the language contribute to the world-view embodied in this passage. One is the prevalence of negation and paradox. The passage is full of explicitly or implicitly negative words: 'dismantled', 'cheerless', 'unlovely', 'unsightly', etc. Paradoxes are salient: the walks are not walks because they are overgrown with grass; the grass is not grass because it is not green; the crop is a crop of noxious nettles (this would be less striking for a reader who knew that nettles used to be cooked, and brewed into tea!); fittingly, it is a garden which denies the expected values of vitality, productivity, brightness—a garden of death. So the actions and motions which are ascribed to the trees and weeds and other objects are fruitless, even destructive; this paradox of actions which are goalless compounds the paradox of a world in which humans are inert, and inanimate things move of

their own accord. Finally, many of the destructive processes are
not assigned an agent or cause: there are quite a number of passive past participles denoting actions but with no specified
agent—'dismantled', 'pieced', 'shattered', 'broken down',
'doddered' (?), 'cracked', 'coaxed', 'worn', 'tattered'. By
whom, or by what? These unexplained processes, added to the
unnatural quasi-human activities of the plants and the furniture,
increase the portentous and threatening atmosphere of this
world. Or rather, of this world-view or mind-style, for what
Maturin is doing is making his language construct a point of view
which systematically transforms our commonsense world into
one which is negative, perverse, and portentous: a world over
which humans have little control, and little understanding of the
controlling forces. This is obviously a technique for defamiliarization; it requires the reader to set an unusual perception of
the world against his own habituated assumptions about loose
wainscotting, plants blown by the wind, or the comforts of the
hearth. The dominant transitivity patterns of this passage reverse
our assumptions about human control over a secure and comprehensible domestic world.

It must be acknowledged that the distinctiveness of this text does
not lie merely in the foregrounding of inanimate agents and inanimate experiencers. This pattern interacts with other estranging
structures such as the negatives and paradoxes; the surreal separa-
tion of the eye from the beholder; the bizarrely assorted references
at the end; the hints of archaism in the vocabulary ('verdure',
'garniture'). Above all, what I called the 'alertness' of this style
comes from complications *within* the basic transitivity structure.
There is progression from the more to the less familiar—weeds
after all are living things which can easily be imagined moving, but
grates, seats, and clocks are much more startling candidates for
human qualities. Then there is the fact that the mental state predicates attached to the objects are not all drawn from the gloomy
or sensational vocabulary of Gothic: 'cheerless' and 'sullen'
perhaps are, but the majority of these state predicates work more
delicately: 'capricious', 'unconscious', 'crazy', etc. These anima-
tions progressively prepare for the strikingly complete humaniza-
tion of the clock as a dumb time-keeper.

A comparison with some simpler and more stylized passage of
Gothic would have been instructive here, if there had been room.

The Gothic mode became enormously popular in the late eighteenth–early nineteenth century, and is still recognizable in much
popular romantic fiction today. It relied on few distinctive features (mostly the use of non-human subjects with human verbs,
and a characteristic vocabulary of architecture, landscape, and
morbid sentiment) and rapidly became stilted and formulaic. We
have glanced at the effects of such stylization in the case of
eighteenth-century landscape poetry (pp. 50–1 above): the
language—hence the mind-style—became habitual and uncritical. It is exactly this cognitive degeneration of the Gothic style
that Jane Austen satirizes in *Northanger Abbey* (published 1818
but probably written twenty years earlier): Catherine Morland's
expectations about life at the Abbey are absurdly distorted by her
reading of sensational Gothic novels, a gullibility which earns
her a parody-Gothic teasing by Henry Tilney in Bk. II. Ch. 5.

The passage just analysed might be described as 'abnormal' or
'deviant' in language and mind-style; in a sense it is, but we must
carefully qualify the implications of calling it such. First, it
is unusual—somewhat original—by comparison with many
works in its genre, and so potentially defamiliarizing for con-
sumers of the genre. Second, it embodies a theory of causation,
and a classification of agents, which departs from certain deeply
held assumptions about the power of humans and the ineffec-
tuality of inanimate objects. That plants do not move because
they *decide* to do so; but that we humans can deliberately cause
them to move, are two aspects of a very basic lesson that all
babies must learn. Does this mean that there must be a mind-style
of 'normal' causation in relation to which the style of *Melmoth
the Wanderer* is a kind of deformed antithesis? By no means. A
style which foregrounded deliberate human actions might also
seem unusual; we will look at such a case in a moment.

A crude contrast of normal versus abnormal does not completely explain the particular impact of a specific text. While
*Melmoth* is undoubtedly odd ideationally in its theory of
causation, its overall character is derived from other circumstances as well, specifically the place of the text in the system of
other, relevant, modes of discourse. It is situated historically and
socially, as well as cognitively, in relation to the dispositions of
the human mind. I will return to this question of the historical
situation of discourse in my final chapter.

Bearing in mind, then, that we should not expect it to feel ideationally neutral and normal, let us examine briefly a text which embodies a different theory of causation. This is a quite ordinary extract from 'Big Two-Hearted River: I', one of Hemingway's stories from the collection *In Our Time* (1924). Here Nick is setting up his solitary camp:

1. The ground rose, wooded and sandy, to overlook the meadow, the stretch of river and the swamp. 2. Nick dropped his pack and rod-case and looked for a level piece of ground. 3. He was very hungry and he wanted to make his camp before he cooked. 4. Between the two jack-pines, the ground was quite level. 5. He took the axe out of the pack and chopped out two projecting roots. 6. That levelled a piece of ground large enough to sleep on. 7. He smoothed out the sandy soil with his hand and pulled all the sweet fern bushes by their roots. 8. His hands smelled good from the sweet fern. 9. He smoothed the uprooted earth. 10. He did not want anything making lumps under the blankets. 11. When he had the ground smooth, he spread his three blankets. 12. One he folded double, next to the ground. 13. The other two he spread on top.

14. With the axe he slit off a bright slab of pine from one of the stumps and split it into pegs for the tent. 15. He wanted them long and solid to hold in the ground. 16. With the tent unpacked and spread on the ground, the pack, leaning against a jack-pine, looked much smaller. 17. Nick tied the rope that served the tent for a ridge-pole to the trunk of one of the pine-trees and pulled the tent up off the ground with other end of the rope and tied it to the other pine. 18. The tent hung on the rope like a canvas blanket on a clothes line. 19. Nick poked a pole he had cut up under the back peak of the canvas and then made it a tent by pegging out the sides. 20. He pegged the sides out taut and drove the pegs deep, hitting them down into the ground with the flat of the axe until the rope loops were buried and the canvas was drum tight.

There is one dominant transitivity structure: the majority of clauses present Nick as an agent of a physical action affecting a material object in some way:

2. Nick dropped his pack . . .
5. He took the axe out . . .
7. He smoothed out the sandy soil . . ., etc., cf. 9, 11, 12, 13, 14, 17, 19, 20.

All the predicates designate manipulatory actions literally speaking, i.e. using the hands (which are mentioned in 7 and 8); the objects affected are items of his kit, parts of his makeshift tent, and detailed features of the site. The effect is of close focus on a sequence of precise, small-scale activities. Other predicates emphasize the deliberateness of Nick's actions: 'looked for', 'wanted to', 'did not want', 'wanted'. Purposiveness is indicated in a number of phrases at the ends of sentences: 'large enough to sleep on', 'into pegs for the tent', 'down into the ground . . . until the rope loops were buried'. Apart from these indications of Nick's conscious intentions, there are almost no mental state or mental process predicates—only the straightforward 'hungry' (3). Other state predicates are physical descriptions: 1 'wooded', 'sandy', 4 'level', etc.; only 8 'smelled good' and 'sweet' express Nick's evaluation of his surroundings, and they relate directly to sensory perceptions: in this passage the physical is physical, and not a projection of the character's state of mind. All in all, the passage is minimally introspective and minimally evaluative.

*Syntax* is of a simplicity associated with straightforward narrative. Because all the sentences are declarative, the clause elements Subject, Verb, Object occur most often in the order SVO, the order which is normally associated with the expression of actions in narrative. All clauses are in active voice; there are no passives to disturb the SVO order. The agent (Nick) is almost always the first word or phrase of a sentence; rarely is any other element of clause structure shifted to occupy the first syntactic position (see, exceptionally, sentences 12–14). The sequence of clauses and sentences is organized by *parataxis* rather than *hypotaxis*, that is to say, it is a sequence of clauses of similar status linked by 'and' or 'then' or merely an implied temporal link, with very few subordinate clauses or non-temporal cohesive ties (see pp. 66–7 above). This simple parataxis is *not* neutral, but a definite literary style, traditionally and widely associated with plain, simple, often naïve narration (primitive narrative such as the *Anglo-Saxon Chronicle*, children's stories, etc.). Readers are likely to bring to their response to this passage their experience of other instances of the style, the values which have become attached to this form of syntax in the history of narrative writing.

Interestingly, there is one potential significance which seems not to emerge from this passage. A text which, like this one, contains many transitive SVO structures with human agents, might be associated with a tough, action-packed style. One might imagine that this would be particularly likely to materialize with Hemingway, given his preoccupations and his image; but in this passage, presumably the relatively domestic actions Nick performs cancel any suggestions of energy or violence. This situation is a reminder to the linguistic critic to be cautious in assigning significances to particular linguistic structures without consideration of context and content.

Just as a foregrounding of SVO structures does not automatically mean a mind-style preoccupied with physical activity, so energy and violence might be encoded in some quite different type of structure. Here is an instance, from Dashiel Hammett's *The Maltese Falcon* (1930); the sinister Joel Cairo has just pulled a gun on investigator Sam Spade:

1. Cairo went around behind him. 2. He transferred the pistol from his right hand to his left. 3. He lifted Spade's coat-tail and looked under it. 4. Holding the pistol close to Spade's back, he put his right hand around Spade's side and patted his chest. 5. The Levantine face was then no more than six inches below and behind Spade's right elbow.

6. Spade's elbow dropped as Spade spun to the right. 7. Cairo's face jerked back not far enough: Spade's right heel on the patent-leathered toes anchored the smaller man in the elbow's path. 8. The elbow struck him beneath the cheek-bone, staggering him so that he must have fallen had he not been held by Spade's foot on his foot. 9. Spade's elbow went on past the astonished dark face and straightened when Spade's hand struck down at the pistol. 10. Cairo let the pistol go the instant that Spade's fingers touched it. 11. The pistol was small in Spade's hand . . .

. . . 12. Spade by means of his grip on the Levantine's lapels turned him slowly and pushed him back until he was standing close in front of the chair he had lately occupied. 13. A puzzled look replaced the look of pain in the lead-coloured face. 14. Then Spade smiled. 15. His smile was gentle, even dreamy. 16. His right shoulder raised a few inches. 17. His bent right arm was driven up by the shoulder's lift. 18. Fist, wrist, forearm, crooked elbow, and upper arm seemed all one rigid piece, with only the limber shoulder giving them motion. 19. The fist struck Cairo's face, covering for a moment one side of his chin, a corner of his mouth, and most of his cheek between cheek-bone and jaw-bone.

The point of view is external perspective (pp. 141–2 above). There are very few mental process predicates indicating the protagonists' motives or feelings, or the narrator's judgements (only 9 'astonished', 13 'puzzled', 15 'gentle', 'dreamy'). A few estrangement devices emphasize the conjectural nature of judgements (13 'look', 18 'seemed'). But the externality derives largely from the insistently physical character of the nouns and predicates of the passage. To take the predicates first, they designate actions—4 'patted his chest'—and, to a large extent, movements: either movements of the subject—1 'Cairo went around behind him'—or changes of location caused to the object—2 'transferred the pistol'. These characteristic predicates are so prominent in the passage that it would be superfluous to offer further illustration; but readers are advised to check the verbs one by one to confirm just how movement predicates dominate the text. Now these predicates are accompanied by locative prepositional phrases, and some locative adverbs, in virtually every clause in the extract; 1 'behind him', 2 'from his right hand to his left', 3 'under it', and so on. Some of the phrases indicate movement—6 'to the right'—and the others meticulously document positions—5 'six inches below and behind Spade's right elbow'. Cumulatively, the impression is one of continuous spatial movement within precisely defined points in a small space: to that extent it is like the Hemingway passage, but it is vitally different in other respects. One is the sheer density of movements and directions and locations, and their diversity (as opposed to the essential congruity of Nick's integrated series of purposive actions): these factors produce an atmosphere of frenzied, unpredictable activity in *The Maltese Falcon*. A further, crucial, difference is in the treatment of agency. In the Hemingway extract, of 26 noun phrase subjects, no fewer than 18 refer to Nick as agent. Of 27 in the Hammett, only 10 refer to Spade or Cairo as agents (at transitions in the narrative when the initiative shifts); 13 refer to parts of their bodies *as if* these were agents; the 4 remaining are subjects of state predicates and again refer predominantly to body parts—5 'The Levantine face', 11 'The pistol', 15 'His smile' and 18 'Fist, wrist, forearm, crooked elbow, and upper arm'.

Another relevant statistic is the total number of noun phrases referring to body parts or clothes, that is to say counting those that occur in prepositional phrases, and as objects, as well as subjects. The breakdown of all noun phrases is as follows:

| Humans | 17 |
|--------|----|
| Objects | 7 |
| Body parts, clothes | 47 |
| Total | 71 |

This amounts to a remarkable foregrounding of parts of the body and a backgrounding of the whole human as agent and as consciousness. The impression of frenzied physicality more or less out of conscious control derives from this focus on bits of the body moving rapidly in diverse directions.

I have commented elsewhere on the use of body-parts as pseudo-agents: in *Linguistics and the Novel* I related it to a context of what I called 'alienated sex' in D. H. Lawrence's *Sons and Lovers*. It is also a stock feature of pornography. Once again, we have an example of how the context changes the significance of a construction, though having said that, one might speculate that there is a key, in this peculiar use of noun phrases, to the link between violent and pornographic texts and between their associated mind-styles.

## Notes

1. 'Linguistic Function and Literary Style', in S. Chatman, ed., *Literary Style: A Symposium* (New York and London: Oxford University Press, 1971), p. 332.
2. For a summary of traditional theories of metaphor, see T. Hawkes, *Metaphor* (London: Methuen, 1972); for a stimulating collection of modern essays treating metaphor from linguistic and other points of view, A. Ortony, *Metaphor and Thought* (Cambridge: Cambridge University Press, 1979).
3. Chs. 6 and 7 of R. Fowler, R. Hodge, G. Kress and A. Trew, *Language and Control* (London: Routledge and Kegan Paul, 1979).
4. R. Fowler, *Linguistics and the Novel* (London: Methuen, 1977).
5. See Note 1 above.
6. On psycho-linguistic implications of simplicity and complexity in coding, H. H. Clark and E. V. Clark, *Psychology and Language* (New York: Harcourt Brace Jovanovich, 1977), Ch. 14 is very helpful.
7. See M. A. K. Halliday, 'Antilanguages', in *Language as Social Semiotic* (London: Edward Arnold, 1978), pp. 164–82.

# 11
# Conclusion

I hope it will be clear that this book was written with a theory in mind: a theory summed up in the title of my previous book, *Literature as Social Discourse*. This theory maintains that a literary text, like any other text, is primarily the realization of a mode of discourse (more usually, more than one mode). That is to say, its basis is a way of writing that precedes it and is found more widely than in just the individual work. Whatever is created by the individual writer, it is not the whole being of the text, because nothing is possible without the pre-existing discourse: and that is rooted in social, economic, political, and ideological conditions which go far beyond the consciousness and control of the writing subject, 'the author'. This is not a matter of linguistic *styles* only; styles of discourse encode the systems of ideas of the cultures which produce them. In effect the author is constituted by the forms and the ideas of the discourses which (with their social conditions) s/he has experienced. Creativity is founded on the author's critical consciousness of these resources of discourse, and the practical skill to deploy language to a defamiliarizing effect. Because the whole process of production and reception of texts is essentially historical, defamiliarization must be transient, regularly requiring a secondary application of critical consciousness: the consciousness of the linguistic critic.

In this short book, I have not developed as fully as I might have done the implications of these claims, because of the pressure of other topics. I wanted to introduce the reader to a good range of types of linguistic construction; to visit several useful topics in literary criticism; and to illustrate the practice of analysis by reference to a wide variety of literary examples. None could be discussed very fully, and certainly not set properly in its historical context. In this final chapter I would like to draw together some of the implications of the theory of literature as social discourse; and particularly with reference to the view of the *reader* which the theory suggests.

In settling on the theory sketched above I have made a firm decision against the popular 'objective' model of literary form and of linguistic criticism. That position claims that the meaning and value of a text are directly accessible on the basis of its own linguistic construction; that the significant structures are open for inspection and evaluation within the text. This is, evidently, a very optimistic point of view. Since the relevant structures are 'there', 'in' the text, the critic, if s/he is at all careful and method-ical, can easily extract them by the exercise of an analytic technique. But we have observed—for example at the end of the previous chapter—that, although linguistic structures as such are objective (thus linguistic analysis is tremendously valuable in criticism), their significances in discourse cannot be read off automatically from the text: a semiotic assessment in relation to cultural factors is required. If we turn now to the reader, the implications of the objective theory taken uncritically are equally cheerful: the text can be read and interpreted simply by using one's basic linguistic competence (knowledge of syntax, diction-ary meanings, phonology, orthography). But literature students know very well that this is not true: a text may remain impene-trable even after several readings, though one understands the words and sentences on the page. Non-linguistic knowledge is called for if a full reading of the text, and one which satisfies the professional critical community, is to be attained. This problem may be severe for the student; but it is only an extreme instance of the general situation with reading and comprehension: all compe-tent decoding of a text relies in large degree on the bringing of knowledge which is not *linguistic* knowledge. There is abundant evidence from psycho-linguistic research that comprehension does not proceed from straightforward analysis of linguistic structure, but from a complicated process whereby knowledge of language interacts with knowledge of the world: with what is called 'pragmatic' or 'encyclopedic' knowledge.[1] Indeed, extra-textual information generally takes precedence over linguistic structure in understanding language: we make guesses about what the text might mean, and check and revise these against what the text actually says. An important part of this pre-textual knowledge is our past and ongoing experience of different kinds of discourse. Reading is a very active and constructive process, much dependent on what one brings to the text; it is not wholly

fanciful to think of the reader actively *producing* a discourse
from a text.

   In part this is a question of factual (encyclopedic) knowledge:
knowing about Keats's life and his sufferings, about the systems
of scientific thought that were available to John Donne, the marriage laws and practices in Hardy's time, and so on. But in large
part what is involved is experience of, and acuteness in deploying,
conventional manners of reading particular modes of discourse:
learning and practising ways of reading. Students who are 'stuck'
when Keats's 1820 Odes, or *Much Ado about Nothing*, or *The
Rape of the Lock*, confronts them as part of an examination
syllabus, have not yet learned the range of reading conventions
appropriate to these modes of discourse—conventions which are
of course blessed by the examination system within which the
student is competing.

   One more example from Pope will readily illustrate some of the
processes involved. I choose Pope because of the manifest artificiality, the obvious distance from our twentieth-century linguistic competence, and therefore obvious reliance, for the text's
interpretation, on non-linguistic information. Here is a very
famous passage from the *Essay on Man* (1733–4):

> Know then thyself, presume not God to scan;
> The proper study of Mankind is Man.
> Plac'd in this isthmus of a middle state,
> A being darkly wise, and rudely great:
> With too much knowledge for the Sceptic side,         5
> With too much weakness for the Stoic's pride,
> He hangs between; in doubt to act, or rest,
> In doubt to deem himself a God, or Beast;
> In doubt his Mind or Body to prefer,
> Born but to die, and reas'ning but to err;           10
> Alike in ignorance, his reason such,
> Whether he thinks too little, or too much:
> Chaos of Thought and Passion, all confus'd;
> Still by himself abus'd, or disabus'd;
> Created half to rise, and half to fall;              15
> Great lord of all things, yet a prey to all;
> Sole judge of Truth, in endless Error hurl'd:
> The glory, jest, and riddle of the world!

                                        (Epistle II, 1–18)

These lines recapitulate an extended argument in Epistle I to the effect that man, in the hierarchical order of things, is paradoxically placed between the higher rational beings (God, angels) on the one hand and the beasts and inanimate objects on the other: man's make-up contains elements from both the higher and the lower ranges of the hierarchy. These are contradictory elements, and Pope's verse builds a picture of man as anomalous and vulnerable because of the contradictions.

The summary which I have just given is very awkward because its content is not really expressible outside Pope's eighteenth-century verse discourse. One problem of the précis is that modern academic prose cannot accommodate the ideas with which Pope is juggling. I felt like putting everything in 'scare quotes': 'hierarchical order of things', 'man', 'God,' etc. The difficulty of expression in modern prose is not simply that atheism and feminism have prohibited these terms, but that the whole system of cosmological and metaphysical beliefs presupposed by Pope's poem is not ideationally encoded in any contemporary mode of discourse which we habitually experience. The modern reader of *An Essay on Man*, therefore, needs to become familiar with seventeenth- and eighteenth-century discourse on 'the great chain of being' and other relevant concepts.[2] More specifically, the modern reader has to be able to cope with the unfamiliar verse form. For example, the discipline of rhyming pentameter couplets requires, among other linguistic constraints, syntactic inversions which could throw any reader who did not expect them completely off course. In the first line, the word 'God' must be parsed as the object of 'scan'—which is not possible in modern English. A reader who had not internalized this rule of eighteenth-century verse syntax would be tempted to misconstrue the whole line and so the ensuing argument. A correct parsing settles the meaning of 'presume' as 'be presumptuous', not 'assume'. It also establishes a contrastive parallelism between the words 'thyself' and 'God' which occupy equivalent stressed positions in the two halves of the line. Here we encounter a major linguistic system which characterizes this mode of discourse: the use of parallel rhythmic positions to effect contrasts and other links of meaning (recall 'husbands' and 'lap-dogs'). Rhymes are also significant: 'scan . . . Man' summarizes the first two lines; 'rest . . . Beast' in 7–8 is part of a little symmetry—

$$\begin{array}{ccc} \text{act} & : & \text{rest} \\ \downarrow & & \downarrow \\ \text{God} & : & \text{Beast} \end{array}$$

—by which Pope implicitly defines man's predicament in terms of initiative versus passivity. Such formal devices of contrast and linkage are a major dimension of the meaning potential of this mode of discourse. Pope's 'ideal reader' must be continuously alert to them and to their significances. He utilizes them in every line throughout the text to shape his theme, to give a specific structure to his argument. This parallelistic verse form encodes a binary, oppositional, mode of thinking which transforms the linear, stepped structure of the 'Great Chain of Being' into a system of contrasts in which man always occupies the disadvantaged position. The main theoretical point to note here is that the form of the discourse actively influences the logical structure of the argument[3]—an insight that Pope seems to have been conscious of, for he writes in the prefatory note to the poem of the advantages of writing in verse rather than prose: not only memorability but also 'force', 'conciseness', 'precision', an unbroken 'chain of reasoning'.

The Pope example demonstrates the historicity of the practice of linguistic criticism if done thoroughly. The modern reader has to work out what values to associate with the unfamiliar structures of a mode of discourse of nearly three hundred years ago, and that in itself is a considerable exercise in the history of ideas and the social semiotic of a past era. But more is involved, because the theory of defamiliarization encourages us to make ourselves aware of parts of ideology that were under question, unstable, changing at a given time: to what extent was the 'Great Chain of Being' problematic for Pope? And more still is required in linguistic criticism, for there is the question of why and how Pope is read in the latter part of the twentieth century. The conventional answer, that great works of art survive because they treat matters of timeless importance, just will not do, as anyone who has thought about Pope in the light of contemporary social assumptions, or, say, Shakespeare in relation to current sexual ideologies, will rapidly realize. There must be a multiplicity of answers to such questions, all involving complex and subtle ideological relationships.

The complexity of these discursive processes, even when no

great historical distance exists between the period of writing and the period of reading, was wonderfully illuminated by one student when we were discussing in class the Hemingway passage treated in Chapter 10 above. I had, as above, contrasted it with *Melmoth* from the point of view of transitivity, and raised the question whether we should regard the one as neutral and natural and the other as deviant and unnatural. This question was of course designed to elicit the theoretical insight that no matter how 'natural' in appearance, language always invites the reader to construct a *version* of reality. The person who took this question on board commented that the Hemingway transitivity, the foregrounded patterns of goal-directed activity, was indeed a construct: and she referred it to the myth of 'the American Dream', the drive in that country to mould and exploit the land for man's purposes, and the peculiarly manipulative and aggressive role of the male in the conquest. Now this is an empirical thesis: writings of that period could be examined for corroboration, and, if it turned out that these transitivity patterns did commonly serve the ideological functions proposed for Hemingway, we would be interested in looking for further evidence of this mode of discourse in other, comparable, conditions. (As Benjy's discourse consists of linguistic selections elsewhere associated with naïve or defective consciousness: see p. 153 above.) Then there is the question of whether these values are simply reproduced by Hemingway, or whether they are problematic and critically defamiliarized. On this question, it was suggested that we might look for the presence and the effects of linguistic structures distinct from the purposive, male, Agent–Action–Goal dominant paradigm. Are there, for example, 'female' structures, say adjectives indicating reflective mental processes and judgements, troubling the uniformity of the general pattern and drawing attention to an alternative mind-style which has *not* been quantitatively foregrounded? Armed with this hypothesis, one could easily go back to the whole story and check; perhaps the reader would like to do this.

Finally, the third question I raised hypothetically about Pope and his modern readership may be considered in relation to the Hemingway extract: why and how does a reader who is sociohistorically distinct from Hemingway's contemporaneous 'implied readers' reconstruct such a discourse? The point about this case is that Hemingway's insistence on males organizing the world has become a widely unacceptable attitude today; and thus the linguistic coding of it has become highly salient for modern readers—particularly for women, presumably. Modern readers have reconstituted Hemingway's text as a different discourse, insisting on its significance within the framework of today's social semiotic for sex roles.

Let us return to a more general consideration of the role of the reader. The approach taken in this book chimes with other contemporary literary theories in giving a privileged position to the reader.[4] Who is 'the reader', who the 'we' I have so frequently invoked in this book? Certainly I do not intend or advocate a purely subjective notion of the reader: every individual reader licensed to respond to and interpret texts according to their personal fancies. Individuals do of course respond subjectively, but the practice of literary criticism is to engage in discussion towards agreement on interpretation and judgement; where disagreement persists, critics generally occupy differing positions within one overall framework of debate. Thus critical response is not subjective but intersubjective, something worked out within a community, and going beyond the level of the individual subject's consciousness. 'The reader' whom I have invoked is a participant in and representative of this process within a literary community (and of other processes) and is therefore genuinely 'we'.

Some theorists of literature have attempted to explain the qualifications of a reader of literature on the basis of the linguist Noam Chomsky's notion of 'linguistic competence.' Linguistic competence is the knowledge which all speakers of a language possess which counts as knowledge of the language strictly speaking. This apparently banal definition makes sense in terms of the restrictions Chomsky places on it: what he excludes. Linguistic competence is highly abstract knowledge of syntax, phonology, and semantics which is commonly shared by all mature, fluent, native speakers of a language. Linguistic competence does not include the many extra factors which come into play in concrete use of language—the socio-linguistic ability to match an appropriate style to a context, pragmatic processes in the interpretation of discourse, and so on. It is this limited linguistic knowledge which is the subject of grammatical description; this knowledge, rather than the actual observed sentences of a language. Chomsky sees speakers as working creatively with their linguistic competence, deploying a finite resource of knowledge to produce and understand a potentially infinite number of novel sentences. This definition of linguistic competence has been widely criticized in recent years, and it is clear that facilities other than grammatical knowledge are used in production and comprehension; but I have simply wanted to present the basic original position on which the literary analogy is based.

The argument put forward by theorists such as Jonathan Culler is that readers of literature possess an analogous skill called *literary competence*.[5] As linguistic competence is knowledge of the properties of sentences, so literary competence is knowledge of the nature of literature and so of the properties of literary texts. Equipped with this knowledge, an author can write, and a reader can read, texts *as literature*. Culler demonstrates what such reading entails by showing how a literary-critical interpretation of Blake's poem 'The Sunflower' differs from a commonsense paraphrase of the words and sentences on the page: literary competence directs us to read for metaphor, symbolism, allegory, significances communicated by indirection. Now it is certainly true that people who have enjoyed a literary education, and/or have plenty of reading experience, can make distinctive special statements about texts which are classified as 'literary', statements which would never occur to people of a non-literary background. The question is whether there is some single, universal, literary competence which is the same for all readers in all periods, and which works equally for any genre of literature. I have argued in *Literature as Social Discourse* that there is not. It is an empirical fact that the formal linguistic characteristics of 'literary' texts vary enormously; and so do the circumstances of their production and reception. What is more, the texts that count as literature vary from age to age—works and authors being admitted to or expelled from the canon—and this is one facet of a general changeability in the reception of literary works. The examples already briefly discussed in this chapter show how readers of different periods constitute texts as different discourses: 'literary competence' must vary from age to age. It also varies at any single point of time: groups of people from different sub-communities within a whole language community respond differently to particular texts. A dramatic example, for me, was when I served as a GCE A-level[6] examiner in English both for students educated in British schools and for candidates from Malaysia and from the Caribbean. Systematically different kinds of answers were furnished by different groups of candidates, varying no doubt in accordance with differences in their educational and cultural milieux.

Anyone who has had experience of the variability of literary response among groups of educated people will realize that 'literary competence' is not one single skill but is variable relative to cultural circumstances. This is to be expected, for two general reasons. First, literary education takes place within a precise social, economic, and political context. In Great Britain, for example, students are introduced to a standard canon of accepted English literary texts (from Chaucer to Ted Hughes) from an early age in primary school. Then they are worked through a hierarchical, and very selective, sequence of public examinations —GCE O-level at 16, A-level at 18, university degree at about 21, perhaps advanced study or research after that. At each stage, only a small minority passes through, so at the end of the process an élite has been selected: this is the source of teachers for coming generations, and thus the process is reproduced historically. The selectivity of the process also ensures that the majority of the population do not have access to or practice in the reading of literary modes of discourse. The overall point is that both groups, the included and the excluded, as well as the different levels of more-or-less qualified people in between the extremes, obtain their discourse competence within an educational system: and an educational system is very much the product of the economic, political, social, and ideological conditions of its time. So the literary competence we acquire changes as historical conditions change.[7]

I mentioned *two* general reasons for the cultural relativity of literary competence. The second is, quite simply, that, if we define literary competence in terms of knowledge of modes of discourse, then its acquisition is just a particular instance of the acquisition of socio-linguistic competence generally. The educational practices which I sketched above illustrate how different groups of people acquire knowledge of different discourses during the process of socialization. The same principles apply as we acquire experience and expertise in the multitude of other modes of discourse which structure the culture: the various languages of the classroom, the media, the law, commerce, entertainment, advertising, family conversation, and so on. These socio-linguistic varieties are what Halliday calls *registers* and what I call modes of discourse (see above, p. 150). It is an elementary fact about socialization that, as people grow into and are moulded into the society they inhabit, they acquire active or passive competence in a vast range of these linguistic varieties, each with its own distinct semantic possibilities. People's socio-linguistic repertoires differ considerably, according to the nature of their roles and relationships in society, and the details and the breadth of their experience and activities. A journalist will have a different repertoire from a doctor: the former must be able to write in the house style of his newspaper, while the latter must be capable in the special discourse doctors use in interviews with patients. This mode of speech is expected by society and especially by its unwell members: indeed it is part of the definition and the qualification by virtue of which a person counts as a doctor. Of course doctor A and doctor B are likely to have different linguistic repertoires according to their individual social and professional affiliations. Journalists and doctors alike—journalists particularly—can be expected to include some degree of literary competence within their socio-linguistic abilities. The journalist may well have passed through a literary education, and certainly works with books as part of his job; the doctor has been exposed to literature through having been long at school and at university (though not *directly* educated in literature), and continuing knowledge of literature is (like theatre, painting, and 'quality' newspapers) part of the means by which the doctor maintains his social position in the professional middle class.

These brief and highly simplified examples illustrate how knowledge of literary styles fits readily into the overall socio-linguistic abilities of individuals; and how this knowledge is, like other knowledge of discourse, part of the process of socialization and social reproduction. Quite simply, the competent reader of literature, through participating in the educational and social processes described above, has come to possess knowledge of 'literary' varieties of discourse within her or his socio-linguistic repertoire—and the various systems of ideas that go with these linguistic varieties.

Let us finally return, briefly, from the reader to the critic and the student critic. The critic's task is to comprehend texts as discourse: to realize them as transactions within society, to understand how they represent the dominant or the problematic beliefs current within a historically specific society. That is to say, linguistic criticism has a goal which is compatible with a traditional aim of literary criticism: to understand the transmission and the transformation of values in a culture. The linguistic critic, unlike many literary critics, is not concerned simply to reproduce dominant values, but to come to a reflexive understanding of the values of a time and a culture. I have insisted that linguistic criticism is necessarily a historical discipline: it must regard the texts it studies not as isolated and timeless artefacts but as products of a time of writing and of a time of reading. The significance of the text changes as cultural conditions, and beliefs, change, and so criticism is a dynamic process.

It follows that the critic's basic qualification is a store of knowledge about the practices and the ideas of the periods which produce and consume the texts to be studied—a historical and social knowledge which was dismissed as irrelevant and improper by the most fervent of the 'New Critics' whose principles dominated Anglo-American literary education from the 1930s to the 1960s. The knowledge that critics possess, and that they study, is embedded in discourses: in documents, poems, treatises, manuals, newspapers, letters, etc., etc. These are the background reading and the research materials for the practising critic. For the student, there is really no shortcut to the amassed experience of discourse and its values which is acquired by the mature critic. But there are some educational practices which foster, and some which inhibit, the relevant experience. Inhibiting are lecture and tutorial teaching formats: lectures encourage passivity in the student and authoritarianism in the lecturer; tutorials promote indulgence and subjectivism when they are the sole medium for the student. By contrast, seminar groups (of say eight to fifteen students) diminish the authority of the lecturer and encourage sharing of experience; they are a classroom model of the *intersubjective* principle of social knowledge of which I have often spoken in this book. In this context, students can pool and compare the range of discourses of their collective experience, and discuss their significance. One of the teacher's major roles is to introduce a good range of varieties of language, so that the authors being studied are seen in relation to other relevant discourse of the time of writing and of the time of reading. It goes without saying that the language studied in the literature classroom should not be restricted to the 'literary'; but the language of 'literary' texts taught in the context of 'non-literary' modes of discourse will feel more accessible, more like a natural part of one's communicative competence (cf. p. 22).

The same principle of teaching literature in a historical context and in the context of a variety of modes of discourse applies to exercises and examinations as much as to classroom practice. A crucial examination in most literature syllabuses is 'Practical Criticism', which requires critical commentary on short texts which are new to the candidates. This exercise was invented by I. A. Richards when he was at Cambridge in the 1920s. In his hands it was a kind of detective guessing game: unattributed and often arcane poems were placed before candidates; those did well who avoided being caught out, making informed and pertinent guesses; the crass mistakes of the others were ridiculed in Richards's book. It was a test to separate sheep and goats. But this test can easily be modified so that it becomes a positive instrument in the development of literary competence in the socio-linguistic sense defined above: all that is required is an examination which contains a socially and historically varied mix of texts (including 'non-literary' ones); with no preference for recherché work or misleading parodies designed to trip up the candidates; all the passages to be precisely titled, attributed, and dated; and the kind of commentary expected of candidates to be requested in technically explicit instructions.

Which brings me to my final point about the qualifications of critics, and their education. I said that the basic qualification of critics is a store of historical knowledge—knowledge of the beliefs and values of cultures and periods; and that this knowledge is embedded in discourses. This book has shown, I hope, that the mechanisms of coding of social meanings in discourse are complicated, and by no means obvious on the surface. Hence the need for a technique to analyse carefully the relationships between textual structure and the text's discourse meanings: a technique, a terminology, and a theory best drawn, I have argued, from an appropriate linguistic model. My entire book has been devoted to exposition of a technique of linguistic criticism, and demonstration of how it works. To make the link with the end of my previous paragraph, linguistics is an excellent source of technically explicit instructions—for essays, research projects, examination questions, and topics for class discussion. If you set people to study agency, or cohesion, or nominalization, or over-lexicalization, etc., in a text, you are giving them something practical and achievable to do. What is more, this analysis is not simply a mechanical exercise: guided by exploratory hypotheses, it will lead to a refined understanding of the significances of a text. I conceded in my introductory chapter that linguistics *by itself* is not a discovery procedure (see pp. 5–6): that analysis has to be guided by knowledge and theory. No one becomes a critic simply by learning linguistic analysis; scholarship and sensitivity, wide reading, and membership of a literary culture are called for. But then, no one becomes a critic simply by reading; analytic technique is essential and linguistics answers this need best of all techniques.

## Notes

1. For discussion and references, see H. H. Clark and E. V. Clark, *Psychology and Language* (New York: Harcourt Brace Jovanovich, 1977); H. S. Cairns and C. E. Cairns, *Psycholinguistics* (New York: Holt, Rinehart and Winston, 1976).
2. *The Great Chain of Being* is the title of a pioneering book by A. O. Lovejoy (Cambridge, Mass.: Harvard University Press, 1936) which gives extensive background to this scheme. Selections of contemporary debate on the poem are reprinted in J. Barnard, ed., *Pope: the Critical Heritage* (London: Routledge and Kegan Paul, 1973), pp. 278–316. A valuable critical and scholarly account of the poem is Maynard Mack's Introduction to his edition of the *Essay on Man* (London: Methuen, 1950), reprinted in Mack, *Collected in Himself: Essays . . . on Pope* (Newark: University of Delaware Press, 1982), pp. 197–246.
3. Note that this is not just an organicist evaluation (meaning is inseparable from form) of the kind beloved of the New Critics; the form is, in my theory, not autonomously created in this poem, but a discourse already available to the author, and socially validated.
4. Some important works of various schools are W. Iser, *The Act of Reading: A Theory of Aesthetic Response* (Baltimore and London: Johns Hopkins, 1978); S. Fish, *Is there a Text in this Class? The*

*Authority of Interpretive Communities* (Cambridge, Mass.: Harvard University Press, 1980); N. Holland, *The Dynamics of Literary Response* (New York: Oxford University Press, 1968). For a survey dealing largely with the German school of *Rezeptionsästhetik* which Iser's work represents, see R. C. Holub, *Reception Theory: a Critical Introduction* (London: Methuen, 1984).

5. J. Culler, *Structuralist Poetics* (London: Routledge and Kegan Paul, 1975).

6. 'General Certificate of Education, Advanced Level', a British public examination sat at the age of about 18.

7. Taking this kind of analysis further would lead us to conclude that the educational system is a political 'practice,' a device designed not so much to develop the individual as to preserve the dominant social structure: an 'ideological state apparatus' in Louis Althusser's term. See L. Althusser, 'Ideology and Ideological State Apparatuses', in *Lenin and Philosophy,* trans. B. Brewster (London: New Left Books, 1971), pp. 121–73.

# Further Reading

The following selections of books in linguistics and in linguistic criticism provide general background, and compatible or complementary approaches. For simplicity, specific technical references given in the notes are not listed here unless they are also *generally* useful for reference.

## I. Linguistics

Aitchison, J., *The Articulate Mammal* (London: Hutchinson, 2nd edn, 1983). (A lively, readable introduction to generative linguistics and psycholinguistics.)

Akmajian, A. and F. Heny, *An Introduction to the Principles of Transformational Syntax* (Cambridge, Mass.: MIT Press, 1975). (A reliable practical textbook on transformational analysis.)

Clark, H. H. and E. V. Clark, *Psychology and Language* (New York: Harcourt Brace Jovanovich, 1977). (Comprehensive introductory survey.)

Coulthard, M., *An Introduction to Discourse Analysis* (London: Longman, 1977). (Handy exposition of main topics in discourse analysis.)

Fowler, R., *Understanding Language* (London: Routledge and Kegan Paul, 1974).

——R. Hodge, G. Kress and A. Trew, *Language and Control* (London: Routledge and Kegan Paul, 1979). (Critical essays on various aspects of language as social practice.)

Fromkin, V. and R. Rodman, *An Introduction to Language* (New York: Holt, Rinehart and Winston, 2nd edn, 1978).

Giglioli, P. P., ed., *Language and Social Context* (Harmondsworth: Penguin, 1972). (Useful collection of classic papers on sociolinguistics.)

Halliday, M. A. K. *Language as Social Semiotic* (London: Edward Arnold, 1978). (Important selection of Halliday's papers, concentrating on the social basis of meaning.)

——*An Introduction to Functional Linguistics* (London: Edward Arnold, 1985). (An account of his own work by the leading 'functional' linguist.)

Hudson, R.A., *Sociolinguistics* (Cambridge: U.P., 1980).

Kress, G., ed., *Halliday: System and Function in Language* (London: Oxford U.P., 1976). (Selection of Halliday's earlier writings, with a useful introduction; read in conjunction with *Language as Social Semiotic*.)

Labov, W., *Sociolinguistic Patterns* (Philadelphia: Pennsylvania U.P., 1972). (Selection of his own papers by one of the foremost socio-linguists.)

Leech, G. N., *Principles of Pragmatics* (London: Longman, 1983). (Introductory account of pragmatics.)

Lyons, J., *Introduction to Theoretical Linguistics* (London: Cambridge, U.P., 1968). (Solid introduction to main topics in linguistics.)

——ed., *New Horizons in Linguistics* (Harmondsworth: Penguin, 1970). (Essays by various linguists, including an important one by Halliday.)

Quirk, R., S. Greenbaum, G. Leech and J. Svartvik, *A Grammar of Contemporary English* (London: Longman, 1972). (Reliable traditional grammar with the benefit of modern linguistic knowledge.)

Radford, A., *Transformational Syntax* (Cambridge: Cambridge U.P., 1981). (An account of a more recent phase of transformational grammar than that on which Akmajian and Heny is based.)

Smith, N. and D. Wilson, *Modern Linguistics: The results of Chomsky's Revolution* (Harmondsworth: Penguin, 1979). (Useful and stimulating introductory work; more technical than Aitchison.)

Trudgill, P., *Sociolinguistics* (Harmondsworth: Penguin, 1974). (Readable introduction to socio-linguistics of the school of Labov.)

## II. Linguistic criticism and stylistics

Burton, D., *Dialogue and Discourse* (London: Routledge and Kegan Paul, 1980). (Applies a British model of discourse to conversation and dialogue.)

Carter, R., ed., *Language and Literature: An Introductory Reader in Stylistics* (London: George Allen and Unwin, 1982). (Concentrates on practical analysis.)

——and D. Burton, *Literary Text and Language Study* (London: Edward Arnold, 1982). (Four practical essays.)

Chapman, R., *Linguistics and Literature: An Introduction to Literary Stylistics* (London: Edward Arnold, 1973).

Chatman, S., *The Later Style of Henry James* (Oxford: Blackwell, 1973). (An approach inspired by transformational grammar.)

——ed., *Literary Style: A Symposium* (New York and London: Oxford University Press, 1971). (Excellent and diverse conference papers, including Halliday's important 'Linguistic Function and Literary Style'.)

——and S. R. Levin, eds., *Essays on the Language of Literature* (Boston: Houghton-Mifflin, 1967). (Anthology.)

Ching, M. K. L., M. C. Haley and R. F. Lunsford, eds., *Linguistic Perspectives on Literature* (London: Routledge and Kegan Paul, 1980). (Anthology.)

Cluysenaar, A., *Introduction to Literary Stylistics* (London: Batsford, 1976). (A very attractive introduction in the practical criticism tradition.)

Culler, J., *Structuralist Poetics* (London: Routledge and Kegan Paul, 1975). (A solid and informative discussion of the earlier structuralist approach.)

Epstein, E. L., *Language and Style* (London: Methuen, 1978).

Freeman, D. C., ed., *Linguistics and Literary Style* (New York: Holt, Rinehart and Winston, 1970).

——ed., *Essays in Modern Stylistics* (London and New York: Methuen, 1981). (Updating of Freeman's earlier collection; largely transformational in approach.)

Fowler, R., ed., *Essays on Style and Language* (London: Routledge and Kegan Paul, 1966). (Original essays by various authors; one of the early works in 'stylistics' to provoke controversy.)

——*The Languages of Literature* (London: Routledge and Kegan Paul, 1971). (Collection of my essays.)

——*Linguistics and the Novel* (London: Methuen, 1977).

——*Literature as Social Discourse* (London: Batsford, 1981). (Collection; emphasizes a growing social dimension to my work.)

——ed., *Style and Structure in Literature* (Oxford: Blackwell, 1975).

Hawkes, T., *Structuralism and Semiotics* (London: Methuen, 1977). (Lively and accessible introduction.)

Leech, G. N., *A Linguistic Guide to English Poetry* (London: Longman, 1969). (Incorporates linguistics in a basically rhetorical model.)

——and M. H. Short, *Style in Fiction* (London: Longman, 1981). (Complements Leech, above, but with the advantage of much more recent scholarship.)

Levin, S. R., *Linguistic Structures in Poetry* (The Hague: Mouton, 1962). (Analysis based on Jakobson's methods.)

——*The Semantics of Metaphor* (Baltimore: Johns Hopkins U. P., 1977). (Is metaphor a matter of semantics or pragmatics? Levin tries out both approaches.)

Ortony, A., ed., *Metaphor and Thought* (Cambridge U.P., 1979). (A stimulating interdisciplinary collection of papers.)

Pratt, M. L. *Toward a Speech Act Theory of Literary Discourse* (Bloomington: Indiana U.P., 1977). (Pioneer essay on the application of speech act theory; discusses a number of issues relevant to *Linguistic Criticism*.)

Riffaterre, M., *Semiotics of Poetry* (Bloomington: Indiana U.P., 1978). (Virtuoso analysis of French poetry.)

Sebeok, T. A., ed., *Style in Language* (Cambridge, Mass.: MIT Press, 1960) (Classic proceedings of 1958 Indiana conference; contains Jakobson's seminal paper 'Linguistics and Poetics'.)

Traugott, E. C. and M. L. Pratt, *Linguistics for Students of Literature* (New York: Harcourt Brace Jovanovich, 1980). (Just what the title says; very useful.)

Turner, G. W., *Stylistics* (Harmondsworth: Penguin, 1973).

Widdowson, H. G., *Stylistics and the Teaching of Literature* (London: Longman, 1975).

# Index

action: *see* predicate
Adams, R.:
  *Watership Down*, 90
agent: *see* role, semantic
Akenside, M.:
  'Ode', 50–1, 71
Althusser, L., 181
Amis, K.:
  *Take a Girl Like You*, 153
*Anglo-Saxon Chronicle*, 164
Angus, I., 37
Apollinaire, G., 40, 47
Austen, J.:
  *Northanger Abbey*, 172
  *Pride and Prejudice*, 57, 108, 132
Austin, J. L., 104, 125

Balzac, H. de, 89
Barnard, J., 180
Barthes, R., 1, 34–5, 38
Beckett, S.:
  *Waiting for Godot*, 116–18
beneficiary: *see* role, semantic
Bennett, A.:
  *Riceyman Steps*, 142–3
Blake, W.:
  'London', 77–80
  'The Sunflower', 175
Brautigan, R.:
  *The Shipping of Trout Fishing in
  America Shorty to Nelson
  Algren*, 63, 66
Brecht, B., 47
Brewster, B., 181
Brooks, C., 2, 83, 102
Brown, R., 101
Browning, R.:
  'My Last Duchess', 93–6

Cairns, H. S. and C. E., 180
Carroll, J. B., 37
category:
  natural, 17, 147
  social, 18–22
Chandler, R.:
  *Farewell, My Lovely*, 66, 67, 108

channel, 22
Chase, S., 30
Chatman, S., 12, 83, 167
Chaucer, G., 176
Chomsky, N., 6, 27, 174–5
circumlocution, 133–4, 153–4
Clark, H. H. and E. V., 26, 167, 180
Cluysenaar, A., v, 80, 84
code, 14, 27–31
cohesion, 9, 59, 61–8, 69, 73
Cole, P., 125
collocation, 64–6, 73
competence:
  communicative, 22, 179
  linguistic, 149, 169, 174–5
  literary, 175–7, 179
complement: *see* role, semantic
conjunction, 66–7
Connerton, P., 37
context, Ch. 7 *passim*
  of culture, 88–9
  of reference, 89–90
  of utterance, 86–8, 93–6
convention, 27–8, 148, 170
co-operative principle, 106
Coulthard, M., 104, 125
creativity, 13–14, 26, 40 ff., 168
criticism, Ch. 3 *passim*
Crystal, D., 26
Culler, J., 175, 181

Dali, S., 46, 47
Davy, D., 26
defamiliarization, 8, 37, 40 ff., 66,
  89–90, 105, 108, 144, 153·
  *see also* dehabitualization
DeGeorge, R. and F., 12
dehabitualization, 35
  *see also* defamiliarization
deixis, 57–9, 69, 90–6, 135
deletion, 63
dialogue, Ch. 8 *passim*
Dickens, C.:
  *Hard Times*, 90, 120, 131

187